What the experts say about
Bridging the Achievement Gap
Second Edition:

"It is very important that those of us responsible for millions of children in public schools take personal interest and responsibility for the success and failure of our children. The Second Edition of *Bridging the Achievement Gap* calls all stakeholders to the task of high expectations and results. Without clear objectives and strategies, we flounder and fail our children. As legislators, this book should embolden us to lead and not follow. Our children are depending on us."

— *Dr. Shirley Weber, Member, California State Assembly*

"Rex Fortune is interested in what works, and why we aren't doing more of it. By looking at California public schools where students outperform similar peers at other schools, and asking what those high-performing schools have in common (strong leadership, engaged teachers, involved parents), Dr. Fortune demonstrates that the Achievement Gap is a measure not of the limits of the students' ability, but of the adults' imagination and political will. He offers concrete suggestions for eliminating the Gap, from the politically difficult – changing the state school funding formula – to the heartbreakingly achievable – producing and using systematic, on-going research about what works. No one who cares about equity in education can afford to ignore this clear, powerful book."

— *Dr. Jeffrey D. Armstrong, President, California Polytechnic State University, San Luis Obispo*

"After many years of experience as an educational practitioner and researcher, I have concluded that African American students attend institutions that are structurally ill-equipped to meet their basic academic needs. Any efforts to close the Achievement Gap must focus on system/structural level reform, versus creating new programs. Toward this end, I am excited about the Second Edition of *Bridging Achievement Gap*. Rex Fortune places the schooling structure at the center of his analysis, which is particularly evident in his call to reform legislation through the modification of California Education Code 42238.02 to include all African American students. This bold and critical new step will provide the necessary resources and attention towards African American students. It has the potential to substantively move the needle for outcomes with the hope of finally bridging the Gap."

— *Dr. Edward C. Bush, President, Cosumnes River College*

"Education in the United States falls short compared to other countries. There is a huge gap in academic achievement for American students, but specifically students of color. The question is how and when will we bridge the Achievement Gap? Rex Fortune has identified a plausible solution in the Second Edition. I urge you to read this amazing book, support and join the efforts of educators to identify appropriate "high needs" groups and allow for new laws to implement change. Failure is not an option for our students."

— *Ramona R. Wilder, CEO, Wilder's Preparatory Academy*

"These independent school studies demonstrate the reproducibility of the science and art of Quality Education, which provides a basis for closing or eliminating the Achievement Gap. If we know about the Gap and care about the Gap, then collectively we must act with agency and urgency to eliminate the Gap. These schools verify and provide proof that it can be done – if there is a collective will."

— *Eugene Fisher, Founder, Watts Learning Center*

"By understanding that policy and funding are associated with best practices, teacher and leader preparation programs are able to develop pathways for research such as *Bridging the Achievement Gap*, Second Edition. These pathways facilitate an equitable decision-making process, ensuring educational supports for high-needs populations as with Assembly Bill 2635."

— *Dr. Kristy Pruitt, Director of Teacher Education, Fortune School of Education*

"Through his continued pursuit and passion, Rex Fortune has identified compelling research that can immediately be used by educators to assist in closing the Achievement Gap. Dr. Fortune's book reveals real-world strategies used by current educational institutions that are successfully closing the Achievement Gap."

— *Scott Loehr, Superintendent, Center Unified School District*

"I strongly encourage all who have interest in issues related to bridging the Achievement Gap in our public education system to read Rex Fortune's new book. He highlights the successful practices that many public schools, including charter schools, are implementing to reduce, and in some cases eliminate, the Achievement Gap, and rightly focuses on the need to advocate with greater courage for the kinds of reforms and resources needed for underserved students to access high-quality options to reach their potential."

— *Jed Wallace, President and CEO, California Charter Schools Association*

"Rex Fortune advocates that the state should provide the leadership and resources to schools and school districts to close the academic Achievement Gap by passing AB 2635. This legislation will enable California school districts that enroll African American students who are not poor but are among the lowest-performing students on statewide tests of English and mathematics, to receive funding to address their academic needs, as they do for other high-need students. Supporters of AB 2635 urge the state legislature and the governor to pass this legislation. Dr. Fortune's book describes several schools where educators and parents are already making progress in bridging the Achievement Gap. Persons interested in finding models of promising practices will find *Bridging the Achievement Gap* a 'must read.'"

— *Evelyn Frazier, President, National Coalition of 100 Black Women, Sacramento Chapter*

"This is a great book focused on the dialogue of helping students win. The dialogue talks less about competition and more about collaboration. The essence of the charter school movement was to create a system that would allow for innovation in addressing student achievement in public education. In Chapter 5, 'The Solution' offers educators and parents solutions to closing the Achievement and Opportunity Gaps that have long plagued students of color, whether that student attends a charter school or a traditional comprehensive school. Thank you Rex Fortune for focusing on solutions and not casting blame."

— *Mike Walsh, President, California School Boards Association*

BRIDGING

THE ACHIEVEMENT GAP:
WHAT SUCCESSFUL EDUCATORS
AND PARENTS DO

2nd Edition

REX FORTUNE

with Dominic Zarecki and Rex Fortune III

ISBN: 978-0-692-19540-6(print)

ISBN: 978-1-54393-792-3 (ebook)

Library of Congress Control Number: 2018958553

CONTENTS

Introduction

'How many exceptions are needed to convince?'

In California, no aspect of public education has been more costly, controversial and indelible than the statistical gulf that shows African American and Latino students as performing consistently below their White and Asian peers.

Two words describe this analytic reality: Achievement Gap.

Despite policy interventions, multiple iterations of curricula and billions of dollars spread across public education's broad constituencies, the Achievement Gap has chronically endured. The impact has devastated communities throughout California, with similar failures consistent around the United States (See Appendix, National Assessment of Educational Progress chart).

Given the Achievement Gap's nagging persistency, should we conclude that the manifestations of measurably poor academic performances by two groups of economically disadvantaged young people of color are inevitable? The answer is demonstrably no.

In 2012, I published the First Edition of *Bridging the Achievement Gap: What Successful Educators and Parents Do.* The book was built around 20 tantalizing exceptions to the rule. It described schools that managed to defy conventional wisdom and evidentiary data based on the contemporary measuring sticks of the day, the Academic Performance Index and California Standards Test.

The book examined 20 high-performing schools with exemplary API numbers, from 802 to 960, at a time when the California statewide goal was 800 or better for all schools. The ethnic enrollments at the schools ranged from 21 to 92 percent African American, or 40 to 96 percent Latino. The collective participation in free and reduced-priced meals programs was 79 percent.

Working within those parameters, the 20 schools in my survey attacked the presumptive toughest obstacles in public education and came away victorious. They served low-income neighborhoods. They were largely minority. And they were high performing.

Bridging the Achievement Gap identified and explored classrooms, educators, administrators, parents and guardians. Their common threads included conditions and population groups that defined the Achievement Gap. But there was a twist. These classrooms consistently produced academic results relatively equal to or better than classrooms filled with White and Asian young people.

Clearly, the 20 schools were doing something — or many things — right. Propelled by their success, they designed methods to defy the predictable statistical outcomes that created and perpetuated the Achievement Gap. They were worthy of closer examination.

The findings of the 2012 edition of *Bridging the Achievement Gap* were not entirely surprising. A decade earlier, I conducted research and published similar outcomes in my book *Leadership On Purpose* (Corwin Press, 2002).

My original study focused on 13 California schools with large minority populations. Half of the students were eligible for free and reduced-priced meals programs. The 13 schools had API scores at least as high as the state average, which at the time was 630.

Since my first two books were published, the universe of public education has shifted dramatically in California. In 2013 and 2015, the state made two momentous changes to the way it measures academic progress among young people in its massive education system.

The first change was the elimination of the API and California Standards Test. For years, the API and Standards Test worked in alignment. The annual test provided baseline data for the API and served as a statewide yardstick for student progress. To replace the Standards Test, state officials introduced the California Assessment of Student Progress and Performance, known as CAASPP. The new assessment was intended to serve as a deeper and more comprehensive measurement while replacing the old test. The CAASPP was first administered in Spring 2015.

The second major change was the adoption of the California Common Core State Standards. Common Core's introduction amounted to a restructuring of educational programs for every public school in the state — kindergarten through 12th grade at nearly 10,000 school sites.

To prepare for the variances in Common Core, the more than 1,000 school districts in California purchased updated or new instructional materials and provided professional development training to teachers and school site leaders. Within months, the curricula and instructional practices for California's 6.2 million public school students and 274,000 teachers moved into a new era.

Measurements for academic progress and the methods for teaching the basics of mathematics and language arts have never been static in California. They shift with the times. They move with trends. And while performance tracking and curricula often follow migratory patterns, the results they seek to measure and improve can be resolutely stubborn and sedentary.

Given the recent changes in student assessment and classroom strategies in California, important research questions must be posed and pondered to quantify the outcomes of this latest systematic upheaval — especially in relation to the Achievement Gap.

Among those questions are:

— How will the use of new state testing instruments compare to past trends seen in Achievement Gap data?
— Will there be an emergence of minority schools that stand as exceptions to the persistent trends of relatively low student performance on state tests?
— More specifically, will there be schools with significant enrollments of African American students who are high achievers, poised to bridge the gap between themselves and groups with traditionally high-performing students?

With these questions in mind, I have prepared a Second Edition of my 2012 publication of *Bridging the Achievement Gap.* The updated work uses the latest California performance data and considers the structural changes brought about by the introduction of Common Core. While focusing primarily on African American children, the Second Edition seeks to identify and describe school and family practices associated with high academic performances by students who might otherwise be trapped in the Achievement Gap.

Despite the new directions in assessment and curriculum, the Achievement Gap shows no signs of shrinking (see Appendix charts, "ELA Scores on CAASPP" and "National Assessment of Educational Progress Scores"). By publishing the Second Edition, I hope to inspire urgently needed discussions and remedies, several of which I will touch on at the end of this introduction.

Eleven schools form the basis of my updated study. The school selection differs from the First Edition — the sites explored in the newest work all have predominantly African American student populations, which allows for a more nuanced and detailed review of successful teaching strategies and includes cultural and social considerations.

The updated student performance outcomes examined in the Second Edition are based upon the 2015-2017 California Assessment of Student Performance and Progress. The entire list of 11 schools scored above the statewide CAASPP average in English Language Arts (ELA) for African American students, which stands at 31 percent. Nearly half of the 11 schools were able to reach statewide ELA averages for all students, regardless of ethnicity. Such performances suggest the Achievement Gap may not be as insurmountable as it appears.

For a closer look, consider the English Language Arts and math performance of 12 schools with a majority of African American students in 2017 (see Appendix, "ELA percentage met.") These data break out statewide rankings and similar-schools rankings. The ranks reflect which percentile the school falls into — a ranking of 5 means a 41 to 50th percentile rank statewide, a 10 means a 91 to 100, and so forth. The schools all serve enrollments that are at least 50 percent African American, with at least 50 percent of students eligible for free or reduced-price meals. And notably, the list reflects a blend of charter schools and traditional public schools.

With evidence based upon the most recent state test results, the Second Edition presents arguments for two conclusions that extend the themes from my earlier research. First, decision makers and policy leaders in California and across the United States must attack the Achievement Gap as a resilient enemy. Leaders must recognize that African American students, families and communities carry the heaviest burden and pay the highest price for the Achievement Gap's persistence. Second, there are schools with high enrollments of African American students that defy the Achievement Gap. The challenge is how to inspire the transfer of strategies from these high-performing schools, teachers, staff, administrators, students, parents and guardians to lower-performing schools and communities that are willing to build upon them.

The Second Edition starts with successful strategies — examining the administrators, educators, parents and guardians who meet the Achievement Gap head on and guide their students across it. The work provides descriptions of high-performing schools that serve primarily African American students. Along the way, readers will visit campuses and classrooms. They will meet teachers and parents. And they will learn how successful schools produce student performances higher than statewide averages for other African American students — and in some cases higher than averages for all students in California.

Subsequent chapters synthesize contemporary research on the performance of African American students. Reports are included from EdSource, the Stanford University Center for Research on Education Outcomes, and the California Charter Schools Association Studies on African American Student Performance in Charter Schools. The Second Edition summarizes what other experts say about bridging the Achievement Gap.

A consistent theme in my research involves the role of parents and guardians in education. The adults who live with successful students are anything but passive observers. The Second Edition describes how schools can create Parent Academies, which have become powerful tools for teaching adults ways to help their children learn at home. Many of the best teachers know that the more education-related interaction parents and students enjoy at home, the better those students perform in the classroom.

Finally, the Second Edition provides practical advice for implementing the most promising practices under discussion. One method is through the establishment of a consulting service for schools that wish to incorporate the findings of the research under discussion. A second method is a grander proposal, involving the introduction of legislation at the State Capitol in Sacramento. The proposed legislation would modify existing structures of school finance and governance, with the goal of tackling and bridging the Achievement Gap.

The proposed legislation would amend the Local Control Funding Formula to include the lowest-performing student subgroup — excluding students with disabilities — on the most recent state-administered assessments for English Language Arts or math.

The bill would require school districts that receive funding under the provision to describe in their Local Control Accountability Plans how they would use these funds to better serve the students at the bottom — the young people whose needs and potential for growth are the greatest.

Skeptics may read the Second Edition and argue that the book is filled with handpicked exceptions, and that the examples provided by 11 uniquely high-performing schools are too few and insignificant to warrant serious consideration, much less a legislative remedy. But such skepticism begs a simple question: How many exceptions are needed to convince educators and policy leaders in California that African American and Latino students from low-income communities, blessed with skilled and motivated teachers and parents, can become high achievers?

The Second Edition of *Bridging the Achievement Gap* shows how the scalability of success can begin with one step — a step inside a high-achieving classroom.

One

The Schools:

How to bridge the Achievement Gap every day

An examination of 11 California schools that found success as they overcame the Achievement Gap. The schools are listed in alphabetical order.

Baldwin Hill Elementary:
'My kids are pretty bright'

Baldwin Hills Elementary thrives in a unique and special world. The school, which serves children in kindergarten through fifth grade, operates within California's largest school bureaucracy, the Los Angeles Unified School District. But thanks to its designation as a pilot campus, Baldwin Hills enjoys significantly more autonomy than many other traditional schools. Moreover, Baldwin Hills is a magnet school for gifted and high-ability students from the community.

    The combination of relative autonomy and magnet status allows Baldwin Hills to demonstrate what can happen when thoughtful, caring administrators and teachers combine with highly engaged parents to provide a quality education for children, regardless of economic status, race, and background.

Demographically, Baldwin Hills would appear vulnerable to the Achievement Gap. Students are predominately from low-income households, with 79 percent qualified to receive free and reduced-priced meals. The enrollment roster of 387 children is 67 percent African American and 23 percent Latino. But state assessments demonstrate that the Achievement Gap doesn't exist at Baldwin Hills.

Standardized test results placed the school above California averages for all students in English Language Arts, with 52 percent proficient. Math scores were slightly below state averages with 35 percent proficient. In both categories, Baldwin Hills' African American students significantly out-performed their demographic peers across the state.

The pilot school designation has become an important factor in Baldwin Hills' success. "As a pilot school, we can do what we feel is most responsive to our school's community," said the principal, Dr. Letitia Johnson-Davis.

The pilot designation required staff members to navigate a process similar to the establishment of a charter school. A comprehensive plan describing curriculum, instruction, professional development, staffing, budget, and governance was prepared and evaluated before approval in 2014. Davis arrived at the site during the process.

While the school carries two official location codes – one for the community school and one for the magnet program – Baldwin Hills operates as one entity. Teachers plan and collaborate as a unified staff. Students eat lunch together and share enrichment programs. Most of the magnet students have been tested and identified as gifted, but they tend to live in the surrounding neighborhoods and are largely selected on the basis of teacher recommendations.

Davis takes a hands-on approach to her administrative roles. She places great emphasis on the most essential definition of an educator's job – to teach young people. She said, "I am an instructional leader first. Instruction is a core aspect of who I am and what I bring. I will teach classes to temporarily relieve a teacher or when a teacher asks me to model a lesson. I sit with my teachers to plan and write their trainings regarding a new pedagogy."

The principal gives detailed feedback on lesson plans designed by her teachers. Each new day finds her in the classroom, conducting observations and preparing reflective questions about teacher practices. She visits every classroom at least twice a month, and has continual "professional growth" chats with her staff.

Student performance data is rigorously tracked at Baldwin Hills. The school runs pre-assessment tests in reading, writing, and math every trimester. Common Core State Standards guide the instruction in math and English Language Arts. For science instruction, the school follows the Next Generation Science Standards. Teachers gather in professional learning communities by grade levels every week.

To a large degree, Baldwin Hills' success can be attributed to the collaborative environment and ability of the school to retain experienced teachers. Among the faculty of 21 teachers, many have worked at the site for more than a decade. Some point to 30 years at Baldwin Hills. Davis monitors instruction and student performance with the help of a Teacher Leader for targeted populations that include non-native English speakers, low-income, and magnet students.

Melissa Ali has worked at Baldwin Hills for 16 years. She teaches fourth grade and believes the emphasis on cultural curriculum is a key factor in the school's success. "We use culturally relevant text, so whatever child is sitting in my classroom, whatever their ethnicity or culture is, I make sure that it is represented in what we read, what we study," she said. "I want each student to feel this is my environment, this is my class. I am learning about me."

A remarkable rainbow of diversity was on display in Ali's classroom. Among her 27 students, two were from Brazil, one from Honduras, several from Senegal, Sudan and Ethiopia. "I make a point of making sure that they identify with who they are, and that they have a sense of pride about who they are," she said.

Tracy Pharris teaches second grade at Baldwin Hills, where she has worked for four years. "We use culturally relevant literature, but my focus is primarily making sure they are fluent readers," she said. "I am focused on their reading and their fluency in math. I do a lot of small-group rotation based on the pretest, so I can identify who needs one-on-one assistance. If they are struggling in an area, I can determine it right away and I can assist them, or other students can assist them."

Pharris has introduced technology to her 23 students. The children use iPads and software platforms that allow them to work collaboratively while the teacher focuses on other children. "I think putting them in cooperative groups is very important," she said. "I facilitate. I circulate. My kids are pretty bright."

Ali and Pharris noted the importance of the nurturing environment at Baldwin Hills. They said every student should sense that teachers and administrators care about them and have their best interest in mind. High expectations are essential, because students will rise to meet lofty standards, they said. Communication between teachers and parents is critical, and schools should assist parents with strategies to help children extend their learning experiences at home. At Baldwin Hills, teachers use a program called Seesaw For Schools. Teachers send pictures and messages to parents when students perform well.

Baldwin Hills has multiple methods to engage parents. "As a Title I school, we have a School Site Council, which has parent members," Principal Davis said. "That council has oversight of our Title I funds and makes budgetary decisions around how those funds are allocated. Parents also have a voice in our Single Plan for Student Achievement – a state requirement."

As a pilot school, Baldwin Hills supports a Governing School Council, which monitors the integrity of the pilot-plan directives, mission and vision. Parents on the council visit classrooms. Additionally, parents participate in staff reviews twice a year and join teachers and administrators in the annual summer retreat, where student performance data from the prior year is reviewed and instructional goals are established for the upcoming year.

The school has a parent coordinator, Jheri Murdock, who helps direct classroom volunteers. Murdock has abundant institutional knowledge about Baldwin Hills – she attended the school as a child and sent her two daughters to the campus. She cited the "tremendous trust" between the faculty and parents, and noted that several teachers enrolled their own children at the school.

"Parents know that decisions made here are fair because they affect the staff's children as well," she said.

Another parent, Derrick Louis, has two daughters in the third and fifth grades at Baldwin Hills. He helps other parents and their children with an on-line tutorial service in mathematics. He volunteers for the school's "engineering and robotics" magnet class and models communications with teachers for his own children.

Like other Baldwin Hills parents, Louis has staff cellphone numbers and is in contact with teachers at least once a week. Parents have informal networks and share information about resources and ways to solve problems. "I make an effort to expose my children to others who are successful, such as Mrs. Murdock's two daughters when they returned home on their college breaks," Louis said.

From its engagement of parents to its cultural curriculum and veteran staff, Baldwin Hills has demonstrated a pathway to success within a diverse, low-income community. Can the school's formula be replicated? Principal Davis offered several suggestions. She said everyone must be aligned to the same mission, vision and the value of high expectations for students. She noted students must see themselves as relevant in every aspect of their school day, including culturally responsive curriculum and classrooms. Finally, she said societal traumas should be acknowledged. "We must address children who experience that trauma with culturally responsive procedures like restorative justice, re-enforcement and recognition of who they are," she said.

Baldwin Hills enjoys flexibility as a pilot school, but its superior performance proves that a traditional school – operating under traditional calendars, personnel practices, collective bargaining, and budget limitations – can thrive with a student demographic that too often struggles to overcome the Achievement Gap.

Cowan Avenue Elementary: 'There are no silver bullets'

Cowan Avenue Elementary School is a traditional school that defies traditions. Located just over a mile north of Runway 24R at Los Angeles International Airport, Cowan shatters stereotypes and turns assumptions into absurdities. Statistically, Cowan should be a model for the challenges presented by the Achievement Gap. Instead, the school is the opposite – it excels on all levels. The Achievement Gap has no impact at Cowan Avenue Elementary.

Unlike eight of the exceptional charter schools on our list, Cowan is a traditional public school. It follows the traditional academic calendar, just like other public schools in the Los Angeles Unified School District (LAUSD). Educators at Cowan work under a collective bargaining agreement between the United Teachers of Los Angeles and LAUSD.

The circumstances that typically fuel the Achievement Gap abound at Cowan. Poverty pervades the lives of many of the school's 296 students, 59 percent of whom qualify for free and reduced priced meals. African American children comprise 78 percent of the student body. Another 13 percent are Latino. But when Cowan tests the progress of its students, the assessments reveal young scholars who can compete with the most affluent suburban schools in California. The success – demonstrated by double-digit performance gains in recent years – inspired LAUSD leadership to name Cowan an Excelling Magnet School.

Numbers tell part of the story at Cowan, but they don't explain the school's remarkable success. By the numbers, 62 percent of Cowan's students met state assessment proficiency in English Language Arts, with 52 percent proficient in mathematics. Among the African American children at Cowan, the proficiency rates were 59 percent in English and 49 percent in math – numbers that are significantly higher than California averages for African American students, or indeed for all students.

To move beyond the numbers and understand how Cowan positions itself to thrive, principal Richard Da Sylveira pointed to a simple recipe. Attitude and culture are paramount. There is "self accountability at every level in the organization," he said. Cowan teachers look upon their students without bias. The educators focus on a student's potential, granting no regard to a family's income or social status. Also significantly, Da Sylveira explained how the school uses interim tests from the Smarter Balanced Assessment Consortium to ensure that Cowan students were not surprised by the annual state tests given in the spring. Finally, the school offers frequent testing and uses the resulting data to adjust deliveries of instruction.

In one sense, Cowan is no different from thousands of other schools across California. The teachers at Cowan emphasize Common Core State Standards. But instruction does not rest at the boundaries of Common Core. The school's more experienced educators have their principal's blessing to introduce their own approaches to building academic rigor. Moreover, the educational mission is not dictated by the clock or calendar. If students fall behind, they can receive after-school tutoring for eight to 12 weeks of the year.

As with other exceptional schools under examination here, professional coaching and collaboration play a large role in the Cowan success story. Administrators conduct teacher observations once or twice a week. The professional staff holds weekly grade-level meetings where the teachers discuss strategies and exchange ideas.

Parents also play important roles at Cowan, though parental participation tends to follow a traditional course. Teachers and the principal encourage parents to participate in teacher-parent conferences, and teachers use the ClassDojo platform to communicate with parents, often on a daily basis. Cowan grade books are online and available for parental review of their children's progress.

If a Cowan student begins to fall behind, the school can schedule Response to Intervention or Student Study Team meetings with parents or guardians, and use professional approaches to determine the best course of action. The strategies involve parents, teachers, administrators, and the student. The teams work to identify any specific academic, behavioral, or campus culture problems. Remedies are collectively explored, debated, and agreed upon.

When asked what advice he would offer other school leaders who wish to obtain the results found at Cowan Elementary, Da Sylveira insisted the school has not discovered a magic road forward. He spoke about simple, time-tested pathways and honest, collaborative hard work. The administration has been stable – Da Sylveira has been at Cowan for a decade – and the faculty is loyal to the school and its children.

"There needs to be a single vision, and there needs to be stability," he said. In the case of Cowan, that single vision has been to close the Achievement Gap. He continued, "As the school leader, I have never failed to talk about how African American students fair in school."

Curiously, Cowan remains something of an outpost in its Westchester neighborhood. Da Sylveira noted that while the school's enrollment is almost 80 percent African American, the Cowan

Avenue neighborhood is substantially White. Cowan administrators never complain that local residents choose not to send their children to the neighborhood school. Other parents across Los Angeles see the results and sacrifice time and gasoline to get their children to Cowan.

"Based on my experience, I have concluded there are no silver bullets when it comes to operating an effective school," Da Sylveira said. "It takes a strong team committed over time to a shared vision that the children in their care can be successful. We just have to figure out ways to make it true."

Fortune School: 'Whatever it takes' attitude

They take no classes. They receive no grades. They never graduate. But at Fortune School, parents and guardians are the bedrock of success. They are instantly acknowledged, celebrated and always made to feel welcome. As Odisa Nyong, who served as principal, said, "Parent involvement is the spoon that stirs the pot."

Most high-achieving schools search for ways to integrate parents into the academic, cultural and social environments on campus. If nothing else, parents can help minimize the dramatics at school as students move from childhood to adolescence. Ideally, parents provide early intervention when their offspring struggle academically or socially. Parents add layers of support and discipline.

But Fortune, a kindergarten through fifth-grade charter school on Stockton Boulevard in Sacramento, has made a specific and strategic effort to enhance the relationship between the classroom and the parent.

The effort to create strong bonds between school and home has brought benefits. Fortune School, whose students are predominately African American and Latino, has successfully narrowed the Achievement Gap. On the 2017 California assessments, Fortune students scored 42 percent proficient in English Language Arts and 36 percent proficient in math. State averages for African Americans were, respectively, 31 and 19 percent. Statewide, 49 percent of all students were proficient in English Language Arts, and 38 percent in math.

As is the case with many charter schools, Fortune asks parents for volunteer hours during the academic year. In Fortune's case, the suggestion is 40 hours.

About half of Fortune School's parents and guardians fulfill the suggested time allotment. And many parents far exceed the goal. But Nyong and his team do not allow volunteer hours to set the singular definition of parental involvement. They have other strategies to stoke and sustain interest. There are parent clubs with meeting sessions called "Doughnuts for Dads" and "Muffins for Moms." There is the School Site Council, which fulfills the planning and monitoring requirements for state and federal programs.

In each of these settings, the principal receives positive, informal and informative interactions from small groups of parents. From gossip to the discussion of serious concerns, the welcoming attitude and eager solicitation of parental input has allowed Fortune School to build a reputation for inclusiveness and transparency. Along the way, the parental focus establishes valuable lines of communication among teachers, staff and the adults who maintain supreme influence over the young scholars at home.

Parental involvement doesn't stop at the Fortune School door. A major annual event for Fortune students is a visit to a college or university campus. Parents and guardians serve as chaperones for these visits. Sometimes, the group's arrival marks a parent's first step onto a university campus.

Early in a child's academic career at Fortune School, college tours begin. The students do not wait until their third year of high school to learn college is more than an abstract concept. They do not wait for the standardized entry exams and application deadlines, when many other young people scramble to seek college admission.

Fortune School fifth graders make a two-day trip to California Polytechnic State University, San Luis Obispo. Science professors and graduate students welcome the youngsters. For several hours, they are encouraged to engage in various laboratory activities. The seedlings for the academies of higher education are planted young.

By the time a student reaches fifth grade at Fortune, the parent or guardian is thoroughly familiar with the protocols of involvement. One parent, Tia Pope, described several ways in which her child's fourth-grade teacher presented information about progress in the classroom. Messages came from the software communications app "ClassDojo," which allows sharing of photos, videos, and text. Pope also exchanges emails with her son's teacher.

There are also old-fashioned methods to establish links between the classroom and home. "The teacher sends home Fourth Grade Folders, where my son puts assignment homework and I sign off that I have reviewed the homework," Pope said. She occasionally visits the classroom to observe progress, with encouragement from the teacher. Pope learned the art of after-school tutoring by watching YouTube channels. When her son responds with good grades, he occasionally receives a surprise trip to a regional amusement park.

Frances Funches is a great aunt in her 70s with custody of two Fortune School students. Her presence and activities in the classroom are akin to perpetual motion. She serves on the School Site Council. Whenever Fortune School conducts a parent academy meeting — designed to help adults understand the challenges and mission of education — Funches is present. When parents were offered briefing sessions on the introduction of Common Core State Standards, she was there.

Funches chaperones field trips and volunteers for the Teacher Appreciation Committee. At home, a large bulletin board tracks assignments, awards and goals for Funches' two students. Test scores are posted on the board, and predictions are made as to where the young people will land academically during the next year.

Many Fortune School parents share ideas and strategies to bring classroom success home. They share practices. Some parents move beyond earthly and institutional methods for education and seek assistance from higher sources. "We pray together as we are driving to school," Onae Drayton said. Another parent described how she played church music when the children were tumbling out of bed in the morning. The children sing along. For many parents, religion becomes a vital component of their child development practices.

From proudly secular to intensely spiritual households, parents bring a richness of diversity to the Fortune School experience. Several mentioned the importance of ancillary activities that transcend generations and can not happen without parental or guardian endorsement — Girl Scouts, dance classes, community mentor programs, even an art bereavement camp, which serves students who have experienced violent deaths in their families. The involvement of families runs deep at Fortune School.

None of this is by happenstance. Fortune School was the first charter school established by the Fortune School of Education in Sacramento County. The program began in 2009, designed by Margaret Fortune, who serves as President and Chief Executive Officer of the Fortune School of Education. She is also my daughter.

Margaret has a deep background in education. She was an advisor on charter schools to California Governor Arnold Schwarzenegger, and was the founding Superintendent of St. Hope Public Schools, the organization started by former Sacramento Mayor Kevin Johnson. At St. Hope, Fortune was involved in the creation and growth of Sacramento Charter High School and PS 7, a kindergarten-to-eighth grade school in South Sacramento that will be discussed later in this book.

At Sacramento High, Fortune worked with Odisa Nyong, who was Dean of Students for the St. Hope organization. She respected his work and knew he was expert at implementing the St. Hope philosophy of "Five Pillars." The pillars set basic goals: high expectations, focus on results, more time, choice, and commitment. They are posted in classrooms at all Fortune School of Education sites.

Fortune Schools have protocols for tracking academic progress. "We do weekly assessments in English Language Arts, math, science and social studies," Nyong said. "Then, teachers do data reflections on their students' performance and open discussion at weekly data team meetings to figure out best practices."

For the first two months of school, the principal observes every classroom on a weekly basis. But the principal is not the only person who visits. Administrators and educators from other Fortune schools take time away from their sites to make rotating visits to sister campuses, where they offer constructive feedback to the staff.

From the principal's viewpoint, the strategies embraced by Fortune School are easily transferable to other schools with similar student populations. Not surprisingly, Nyong began with the bond between teachers and parents. He would encourage likeminded administrators, he said, "To help teachers form a high level of trust with their families, and be ready to start this at parent orientation in the beginning of the school year."

From there, Fortune School's winning strategies move from specific to universal. "Help teachers to become masters of their content areas," Nyong said. "And the school leader, teachers and other school staff must have a 'Whatever it takes' attitude."

A tour of Fortune School brings these strategies to life, along with the always-present goal of sending every Fortune student to college. Entering a classroom, the visitor is greeted by a chorus of students shouting, "Welcome to the Class of 2029," or whatever year the age group can expect to graduate from a four-year college, without gap years or interruptions. Then, an individual student approaches the visitor, makes a personal introduction and briefly describes what the class is studying at that moment. The scholar will ask if the visitor has any questions.

Every class chooses a university pennant for display on the door or windows — a "mascot" school to stoke ambitions. Students often write reports about their mascot university. And at Fortune sites, the word "student" is usually replaced by the word "scholar."

Fortune School teachers appreciate the college-bound emphasis and long-range goals. They also appreciate the philosophy of encouraging educators to become experts in their content areas. Teachers are given personal planning time and early release for planning each week. There is also time for grade level meetings among staff, cross grade-level meetings and debriefings by visiting colleagues from other Fortune sites — all of which facilitate the sharing of ideas among educators.

Academic progress is tracked with a program called "Illuminate." The software processes student data and monitors fluency tests, spelling tests and assessments from the start of the year in English Language Arts and math. The assessments are essential because early intervention is a critical part of each teacher's responsibilities at Fortune School.

One educator, Christine Walker, said, "Teachers keep track of fluency on charts, post them on data walls, and talk to scholars about action plans." Teachers identify students who score above 80 percent proficiency on the standardized test assessments. Students who test below the 80 percent threshold are supplemented with appropriate interventions designed to identify their challenges and push them into the 80 percent proficiency category.

Interventions require extra work, and there are no shortcuts at Fortune School. Struggling students are invited to attend additional days of instruction at the end of each trimester, while higher-achieving students take an inter-session break.

During these extra-time sessions, teachers operate in much smaller groups. The sessions, where students are paired with their regular classroom teachers, can expand the academic calendar by more than 25 days. Some students receive more than 200 days of instruction, compared to 176 days in the regular academic calendar. During the extra study sessions, the Fortune School pillar of "more time" becomes tangible, a tool far more valuable than a slogan.

The significance of parental relationships is enhanced when a Fortune School student is identified as low performing. Teacher Shunta Williams said, "I get parents involved. I let them know the importance of the current situation with their scholars. I form small groups — one to three scholars, or one-on-one, for instruction. I give praise and external reinforcers. We encourage them to use YouTube tutorials. We have 'Fun Fridays' as rewards for good work. We encourage them to read what excites them, like Harry Potter books."

Several Fortune School teachers were asked to compose an advice list for colleagues at other sites with similar student populations. The list was comprehensive and direct in its wisdom. It said, "Careful preparation of lessons. Be prepared before facing the scholars. Maintain consistency, so that students know what to expect. Have routines. Encourage your students. Know your students. Have effective classroom management. Use cooperative teamwork among teachers. Have collective goals. Have two or three 'read-alouds' each day. Teacher reads. Students read. This increases fluency. Have daily use of technology, especially for upper grades, and practice tests."

Parents were not singled out on the teachers' list, but they were hovering nearby. At Fortune School, parents and guardians are never far from the essential activity of educating their children, of transforming them into scholars for life.

KIPP Empower Academy:
'A mindset that all students can achieve'

Culture matters at KIPP Empower Academy. The South Los Angeles elementary school places a unique emphasis on creating a campus culture where students are free to express themselves and build not only their academic potential but also their physical health and emotional spirit as well.

KIPP Empower serves children in transitional kindergarten through the fourth grades. Each day begins with "community circles," where students discuss a question of the day and express how they feel about events around them.

Many of the children have experienced significant trauma in their lives, and the teachers and administrators are sensitive to each student's vulnerabilities. The sensitivities extend to student disciplinary measures, where the school provides "trauma informed counseling" to children with discipline issues. Community-based partners assist the educators and help deliver counseling.

The attention to culture and appreciation for the children's environment has helped push KIPP Empower into a category of success that contradicts the Achievement Gap. Despite a demographic profile that indicates significant poverty – 88 percent of the school's 563 students qualify for free and reduced meals – KIPP Empower has produced excellent results on state assessments.

In English Language Arts, 41 percent met proficiency, which was just below the statewide average for all students. In mathematics, the performance of KIPP Empower students was remarkable, with 53 percent proficient, a number substantially higher than the statewide average of 38 percent proficiency.

The KIPP Empower enrollment includes 69 percent African American children and 28 percent Latino students. The results at

KIPP Empower far exceeded the statewide averages for African American children, demonstrating the school's ability to overcome the Achievement Gap.

Surprisingly, the triumphant assessments aren't necessarily celebrated in the principal's office. The KIPP Empower Academy site leader, Chinedu Udeh, was reluctant to grant an interview until her students' scores moved beyond the 80 percent proficiency rate.

Thankfully, the former Teach For America veteran relented and proved eager to discuss the school's culture, teaching methods and parental interactions. Udeh was completing her first year as principal when we spoke, though she previously served as a vice-principal and teacher coach. Her administrative team includes two assistant principals and two deans. Together, they direct 30 teachers.

As the test scores indicate, KIPP Empower has a strong focus on math. Teachers use an "exit ticket" system, where students refer to material they have learned during the school day. Beyond the tickets, educators rely on data-driven instruction. The school follows Common Core State Standards in every subject area, and the administrative team holds biweekly meetings with every teacher.

May is an important month for the professionals at KIPP Empower. The school conducts a "review of standards," led by Udeh and her administrative team. "We examine our scope and sequence of instruction," she said. "We chart out what standards are going to be covered in each unit. Teachers use that scope and sequence for lesson planning in August. The entire school is involved with this. The leadership team plans the training. Each of us takes one subject and models how a lesson should be done. Then we meet together as grade-level teams and do that work for each subject in their grade level."

KIPP Empower is operated by the Knowledge Is Power Program, a national Charter Management Organization founded in 1994 by Michael Feinberg and Dave Levin. The KIPP mission is to provide quality education to under-resourced communities. In 2017, the KIPP banner flew atop 183 schools in the United States, with more than 70,000 students enrolled nationwide.

KIPP was established on a simple premise. The goal was to create an educational baseline in underserved communities that extended beyond a single school year. The baseline would build momentum and propel children throughout their academic careers, from middle school to high school and onto university.

From its birth, KIPP focused on fifth graders. The program emphasized the necessities and rewards of hard work and the absence of shortcuts. Fifth grade was not an arbitrary place to start. It was a strategic choice. Fifth grade became the KIPP entry portal because children entering fifth grade are on the cusp of adolescence, but still sufficiently malleable to form lasting relationships with their teachers and the academic mission. Under the KIPP philosophy, when fifth-grade students understand and accept rigorous expectations, they can glide into the challenges of puberty and beyond with enduring academic foundations.

In Los Angeles, KIPP schools offer transitional kindergarten programs through eighth grade. The regional KIPP headquarters designated KIPP Empower as a "Focus School" for grades TK-4, which brings additional support while KIPP Empower readies children for the all-important fifth grade. The school operates 180 days each year and has extended hours, with daily activities running from 7:30 a.m. to 4 p.m. Some of the extra time is used for small-group instruction.

"Our school uses lots of technology," Udeh said. "In grades K-2, we have 15 laptops per classroom. In grades three and four, each student has a laptop. This enables us to use on-line programs in math like ST Math, MobyMax and Accelerated Reader for ELA."

Another important feature at KIPP Empower is professional development and preparation time granted to educators. Teachers receive a daily 60-minute prep period. The dedicated time is available because other instructors are brought in to teach special programs, such as art, yoga and dance. Every Monday, students are released at

1 p.m., allowing teachers a weekly afternoon for professional development activities.

The school has four teachers for each grade level, and one teacher for transitional kindergarten. An administrator is assigned to each grade level. The grades meet monthly, where the educators dive into the latest data and determine whether corrective actions are required to address student proficiencies.

As for parent involvement, Udeh said, "It is great." In addition to traditional parent-teacher conferences and back-to-school activities, parents attend Family Night and Family Game Night. At Halloween, parents decorate their car trunks. The evening is called "Trunk or Treat." Said Udeh, "Any time we have a program, like Heritage Month, Winter Program, cultural celebrations, Carnival or the Valentine's Day dance, we have tons of parents."

Parent-teacher conferences were underway when we visited. Seated in the lobby, I was impressed by the level of interest shown by parents who were eager to begin their appointments. The school was alive with enthusiasm.

The principal had three pieces of advice for colleagues interested in replicating the success at KIPP Empower. She said, "First, have a clear vision about what the social and emotional support should look like. Second, have a clear vision about instruction. The school should use data daily to decide what the instructional changes should be. Data-driven instruction is very important. And finally, who you hire is also very important. There has to be a mindset that all students can achieve."

KIPP Scholar Academy:
'A prize for what you know at the end'

Music brings magic to KIPP Scholar Academy, a stellar middle school on West Martin Luther King Junior Boulevard in South Los Angeles. Three days each week, the school's entry-level fifth graders receive vocal training and piano instruction. When they complete the eighth grade and move into high school, they can read sheet music and play instruments of their choosing.

"We believe early musical training helps develop the brain, helps kids think creatively and exposes them and gives them a profound appreciation for the richness of diverse cultures," said Tiffany Moore, KIPP Scholar Academy principal. "And when African American boys become involved in music, it keeps them out of trouble. Music seems to help them value school."

Like its sister site KIPP Empower, KIPP Scholar Academy operates under the direction of the Knowledge Is Power Program, a national Charter Management Organization that runs 15 schools in the Los Angeles area and more than 180 sites across the U.S. KIPP Scholar is one of seven L.A. middle schools operated by the group.

In South Los Angeles, KIPP Scholar Academy opened in 2012. The school's enrollment data provides a portrait of the surrounding community. Poverty is pervasive. Ninety-three percent of students enrolled at Scholar Academy qualify for free or reduced meals. African American youngsters comprise 50 percent of the student body, Latino students 48 percent. Enrollment was 389 in 2017.

Despite the hardships and challenges, the results have been impressive for Scholar Academy. It's fair to say the school has essentially bridged the Achievement Gap.

In recent standardized tests — the 2017 California Assessment of Student Performance and Progress — 50 percent of KIPP Scholar

Academy students were proficient in English Language Arts, one point higher than the statewide average for all students. Across California, 31 percent of African American students test proficient in English Language Arts.

Mathematics outcomes were not as powerful for Scholar Academy students, but the results were nonetheless positive. Scholar Academy youngsters scored proficient at 26 percent in math, which was below the statewide total average of 38 percent yet well above the 19 percent average for African Americans. Clearly, the emphasis on music has made an impact at Scholar Academy, most notably in English Language Arts.

At KIPP schools, the days are long. Students are expected in their seats and ready to learn at 7:30 each morning. Classes continue until 4:30 or 5 p.m. Some KIPP schools hold special sessions on Saturday. Many organize summer classes, though Scholar Academy is not among them. Instead, Scholar Academy operates a summer "boot camp" for high achievers, and a summer math program in partnership with California State University Dominguez Hills.

Throughout the school year at KIPP sites, homework is assigned daily. The burdensome workload is driven by the allure of opportunity, said Fineberg, the co-founder, in an interview with journalist Hedrick Smith for the PBS program *Making Schools Work*.

"This is a race. This is a competition," Feinberg said. "There's no prize for winning the race, but there's a prize for what you know at the end. And the prize is that after the 12th grade, those who have the knowledge, skills, and character have amazing opportunities to go off to higher education and learn what they want to learn in this world and get trained to do whatever they want to do."

At KIPP Scholar Academy, the attention given to musical education helps light the path for students. Music serves to illustrate a variety of academic options that students and their families may not have known existed. Professional musicians and musical groups perform at the school. The music teaching staff is comprised of professional musicians who often perform with outside organizations.

Principal Moore has a musical background. And she has professional experience as a teacher at a low-performing school in Los Angeles. In her old job, she was distressed by the minimal expectations that were applied to her students. She wondered if there was a better way. She heard about KIPP, and decided to visit a high performing KIPP school. She saw classrooms filled with students who very much resembled the young people at the campus where she worked. Yet somehow, the KIPP students were performing at much higher levels.

Not long after that visit, a KIPP regional administrator tracked down Moore and asked if she would like to work at a new school — KIPP Scholar Academy. And the offer was for more than a teaching job. She would start as founding principal.

Like all successful schools, Scholar Academy places major emphasis on teamwork. The alliances begin at Moore's office, where an assistant principal, dean, and instructional support coach provide help. The administrators are familiar faces at every Scholar Academy classroom. They visit and observe teachers at least once each week.

Staff support extends beyond classroom visits. "The teachers have a variety of support sources," Moore said. She recited a variety of supplemental opportunities for professional development, including math conferences and an engineering and science partnership with UCLA. Professional development meetings are held at the school twice per month. Moore believes the most valuable activities are ones that, she said, "build the content knowledge of the teachers." She noted, "I would rather make investments in teachers' professional development, than hire new specialists."

Moore invests time and money into professional development and content knowledge for her staff. When the faculty gathers for meetings on subject matter and content, experts in the relevant fields address the team. Often, outside professionals are recruited for presentations.

The nuances of professional development and content knowledge are important, but Scholar Academy also appreciates the value of conveying simple, consistent guidelines to promote the school's culture. The guidelines are built around the word "CORE," which in this instance becomes an acronym that spells out "C" for culture, "O" for organization, "R" for rigor, and "E" for engaging. To spend time with the principal is to hear the word "CORE" repeated and emphasized over and over again.

Technology is critical at Scholar Academy. Each student has access to a Chromebook laptop. As one teacher explained, "By the way, that's the instrument they use to take the state tests, so they get familiar with how to use the instrument on a daily basis as part of the instructional program."

KIPP teachers seem eager to share their success with colleagues, and are generous when asked what advice they would give teachers in other schools about how to improve test scores. Among the answers: "Expose kids to standards with rigor." "Use academic language, always." And, "Teach the way that you would like to be taught."

One veteran educator, Tommy McConnell, has taught algebra at Scholar Academy since the school opened in September 2012. His preference is to work with students in small groups. He believes direct access to teachers and extra attention is fundamental for student success. Small groups also help identify high performing students, who are nudged toward higher-level math courses earlier than their peers. Some students take pre-algebra in sixth grade and move to Algebra I in seventh grade. They wrap up their Scholar Academy careers with geometry in eighth grade.

The goal for these high-performing students extends well beyond middle school. McConnell and his colleagues have prescribed a pathway for their young people to finish calculus in high school and enter college ahead of many other students. The process begins when new student enrollees are directed toward the summer math "boot camp." A major — if underplayed — component of the boot camp occurs when Scholar Academy staff studies new students to identify high achievers in math before the fall semester begins.

McConnell had three pieces of advice for teachers who would like to duplicate the success of Scholar Academy: "Expose students to all standards; you cannot review all year," he said. "Schedule to teach all the standards using the language of Common Core. And give students processes and procedures, not tricks."

Computers — not tricks — play a large support role at Scholar Academy. The school deploys a commercial software program called Illuminate to track student grades, attendance, assignments, regional assessments, and California state assessments. Parents receive weekly progress reports, which provide the opportunity for adults to communicate quickly when they have questions about their children's work.

The importance of the parental role is never overlooked nor underestimated at Scholar Academy. The school operates a Parent Action Committee and a Title I School Site Council. And the traditional transitory path, where students attend school each day and head home in the afternoon, is routinely turned around by Scholar Academy. Staff makes house calls and visits students at home, a protocol that has become an important chapter in the school's success story.

"A major practice now is to visit the homes of all new students in the summer, prior to their attending school," Moore said. "This has had a major effect on improving student behavior and performance in the following school year. In the years when the practice was not in place, there was an enormous amount of time throughout the year spent dealing with the failure of students to adjust to the new school culture."

Engagement between teacher and parent is made easy and convenient. Scholar Academy educators and parents send emails and texts to each other. The school uses a software program to produce the Parent Portal, which churns out the twice-monthly progress reports and quarterly reports.

Parental input is evidenced everywhere at Scholar Academy, from the uniforms worn by students to the food the young people eat. "Parents support the school's uniform policy," McConnell said. "They support the junk food policy. The school has events designed to attract parents, and parents respond to our surveys." However, McConnell noted parent engagement could still be improved, and described it as "an area for growth."

With its emphasis on music and culture and its efforts to identify gifted math students early in their middle school careers, KIPP Scholar Academy has taken substantial steps toward bridging and eliminating the Achievement Gap. In a September 2017 report, the San Francisco Chronicle portrayed the Achievement Gap as all but endemic. The report noted, "Every year, education officials release standardized test scores, and every year they say the same thing: the Achievement Gap persists."

Had the writer ventured down West Martin Luther King Jr. Boulevard in South Los Angeles and visited KIPP Scholar Academy, and had the journalist listened for the musical notes and lyrical sounds of success, the same old story would have reached a different conclusion.

Oak Park Prep Middle School:
'Her magic number is 95 percent'

Classes at Oak Park Preparatory Academy end with something called an "exit ticket." Before students leave for their next class, they fill out exit tickets and post them on bulletin boards. Teachers collect the tickets. They review the work and almost instantly determine whether their efforts from the previous hour hit home or missed the mark.

If the lessons sailed over the heads of too many students, the teachers begin to modify the next day's plan. If at least 80 percent of the class absorbed the instruction, success is declared and the students move forward. Anything less than 80 percent means compensatory action is required — slowing down and backing up.

The exit tickets provide a snapshot on progress and allow for quick adjustments in momentum and direction. As Oak Park Prep eighth grade English Language Arts teacher Rachel LaDue said, "It's definitely a day-by-day task, looking at the data to see what happens next."

Exit tickets and data reviews are among several innovations found at Oak Park Prep, a middle school for seventh and eight grade students in Sacramento. Founded in 2012 as a feeder program for Sacramento High School — the two St. HOPE Charter Management Organization schools share the same historic urban campus — Oak Park Prep was created from the results of a one-year study by Paul Schwinn, who became the middle school's founding principal.

During his yearlong survey, Schwinn visited numerous charter schools. He interviewed teachers, students, parents, staff, and administrators. He focused on best practices. Simply, he was eager to identify which strategies and methods made some programs more successful than others.

Armed with his inspirations for success, Schwinn wrote the charter petition for Oak Park Prep. Soon thereafter, he greeted the first class of seventh graders. A year later, Schwinn was named principal at Sacramento High. Veteran educator Annie Cervenka became principal at Oak Park Prep.

Oak Park Prep enrolled 138 students for the 2016-17 school year. The young people reflected the community around the school, with 56 percent of the students African American and 29 percent Latino. Free and reduced meals were available to 85 percent of the students.

The numbers may be typical for urban campuses, but Oak Park Prep has defied the Achievement Gap. For the 2017 California standardized assessments, 45 percent of the school's students met or exceeded proficiency in English Language Arts, compared to 49 percent statewide. In math, 42 percent were proficient or better, compared to 38 percent statewide.

African American students at Oak Park Prep succeeded beyond all statewide averages for their subgroup. They scored 35 percent on proficiency in ELA, against 31 percent statewide. In math, 34 percent of African American students at Oak Park Prep met or exceeded proficiency, compared to 19 percent statewide.

Closing the Achievement Gap requires a capacity for risk and innovation. As the exit tickets illustrate, new ideas are welcomed at Oak Park Prep. Consider the school's master schedule. Two English and two math classes are programmed each day. The first class sections are taught in the morning. They support objectives built around grade-level expectations. The second classes are offered in the afternoon. They are organized in groups based on specific student needs. The smaller afternoon groups may blend students from seventh and eight grades who encounter similar difficulties with lessons. One group may be busy reviewing long division. Another works to solve linear equations. Some groups are based on reading ability.

Managing a wide range of students' needs in a single class can be difficult for an educator. Oak Park Prep addresses the teaching challenge by sharing the work load and limiting class sizes. For the afternoon courses in English and math, two teachers and an aide typically work together, assisting each other across groups of four or five students. The collaborative environment allows educators to focus more on foundational skills.

The dual arrangement of two English and math classes each day supports a cornerstone of Oak Park Prep: the promise to the school's families to provide more time for instruction. Of course, extra time cannot be contrived — it must be carved away from an already busy schedule. In this case, the extra time is gained by extending the clock beyond the instructional hours offered at most traditional schools in the Sacramento area.

At Oak Park Prep, classes begin at 7:30 a.m. and end at 3:30 p.m., which can be long days for middle school students. The days are even longer for teachers, who remain on campus until 4 p.m. twice a week for professional development and spend two additional afternoons with time dedicated for tutoring students who need personalized attention.

For students, the extra hours are filled strategically and with attention devoted to their unique situations. By providing more time for academics, Oak Park Prep teachers tailor instruction to each member of the classroom. "For students who have already mastered a skill that I am teaching, I'll offer that student extra challenge questions, which are usually extra-credit options," said Ronnie Chavez, a seventh grade English teacher. "I will also differentiate the exit ticket the next day if I notice more than 80 percent of the students have mastered the skill OK."

Most of the work in the afternoon English and math classes is done on Chromebook laptops. High-performing students are guided into high school-level work. A visitor notices two students who finished their tasks quickly in a math "B" class. They grabbed a workbook for the SAT college-entrance exam and began to tackle new exercises. Their teacher previously assigned the SAT prep book, noting the students' eagerness and aptitude.

English and math are emphasized at Oak Park Prep, but the school's curriculum is diverse. Students receive daily instruction in science and humanities. Electives are taught once per week. Students largely design their own electives, based on their key interests. The subjects are broken into workable classes, and every teacher takes one. The school has a running class, a talent show class, an arts class, and a computer coding class. The selection changes as students arrive and depart from their two-year enrollments. Some years, cooking class is an elective. Other years, Spanish is taught. The students establish the lineup, and the teachers deliver the knowledge.

While students get hands-on experience with their Chromebooks each day, they also grow comfortable with the tools and technology that will deliver their annual state assessment tests, reducing if not eliminating the stress that would come from unfamiliarity. English, science, and humanities textbooks are downloaded onto the computer. Teachers have interactive education software and Smart Notebooks, which allow for projections onto a screen viewable by students.

Tracking student progress at Oak Park Prep is a perpetual chore, but the linchpin of tracking is the quarterly assessment. English teachers Chavez and LaDue quantify their quarterly reviews of student progress by using tests similar to state assessments. Students spend three to four hours over two minimum days taking the tests each quarter.

Teachers follow a baseline — a robust data analysis template that they align with every student's performance on the standardized tests. They establish how well each student does on every question. And they reflect, asking themselves, "OK, what worked in Quarter One, or what do we need to fix in Quarter Two?" They create benchmarks against which they can measure student progress throughout the year.

Supporting the work is the principal, Annie Cervenka. She oversees personalized growth goals created for every student at Oak Park Prep. She tracks a variety of performance measures — benchmark academic data, suspension data, and attendance data. Her magic number is 95 percent.

Cervenka, a former science teacher who was recruited to Sacramento from a charter school in Los Angeles, maintains a data file called "State of Oak Park Prep." The file informs her weekly check-ins with every teacher and helps her create groups at the end of each quarter's benchmark assessment period.

Throughout the day, the principal keeps moving. She observes every teacher from 20 to 40 minutes per week. Her observational protocols include notes of teacher actions and student actions. She shares her notes with teachers during their regular meetings. She reviews the exit tickets, and follows up on actions designed to help students who fall below the 80 percent proficiency goal.

Together with Oak Park Prep's vice-principal and office manager, Cervenka has designed an observation template called "Teach Boost," which creates brief reports on each teacher within categories called "Glows and Grows." As the name suggests, the Teach Boost reports deliver compliments and identify areas for improvement.

Another important pathway to success at Oak Park Prep involves interaction with each student's family. Teachers are encouraged to build working relationships with parents and guardians, and to keep them updated on all aspects of their young person's progress. The school gives each teacher a cell phone, and parents receive the phone numbers to call or text.

Each week, a "Green Folder" is sent home with students. The folder contains grades, behavioral reports, a newsletter, and other relevant notifications. Parents are expected to review, sign, and send the folders back to school. Teachers report about 50 percent compliance with the weekly signatures. Some parents prefer to connect with teachers electronically, using the communications program called ClassDojo. About 65 to 90 percent of parents communicate via the Dojo platform, according to Oak Park Prep educators. "Rarely do I have a parent not respond," one teacher said.

Parental attendance at many school events ranges from 25 to 40 percent, teachers estimated. Some teachers offer incentives to parents, such as a "Free Dress Day" pass, which allows a student an excuse from wearing the mandated Oak Park Prep uniform for one day.

Cervenka maintains close watch over the interaction between parents and her staff. She considers the Green Folders an important tool for building relationships and keeping parents informed. She also encourages special meetings with families if a student has unusual problems. Oak Park Prep parents are reliable partners when asked to help intervene, Cervenka said, adding parents make strong showings at special events, including Back To School Night, student-led conferences, oral history performances, and talent shows.

When the principal was asked how she would advise a site leader wishing to replicate the success found at Oak Park Prep, she made three key points: "Spend 75 percent of your time on academics — focus on learning. Make sure your teachers have a roadmap toward student improvement. And do what you can to retain the teaching staff over the years. Make sure they feel challenged and supported."

Her list complimented a series of questions posed by Oak Park Prep teachers when asked how they would help to guide colleagues at a struggling school. The educators identified six essential questions for teachers to ask themselves:

1. Do you have assessments that you work from backwards?

2. Do you have a clear objective that you work on every day?

3. Do you use reflective data, where there is an examination of each question on the benchmark to make sure that each student has reached the benchmark?

4. Do you focus on classroom culture and teach culture from the first week of school?

5. Have you formed groups of students for instruction based on their needs?

6. Do your students move from class to class in the morning as a cohort? And, are they regrouped in the afternoon, based on common needs?

To attain the success at Oak Park Prep, the answers should all be affirmative.

The Sacramento middle school leaves very little to chance when it comes to the academic progress of its students. There is no cheerleading or chanting to exhort how "every student can learn." Instead, the focus is on a methodical, purposeful strategy of collaboration and results, driven by an evidence-based culture and exemplified by the simplicity of an exit ticket.

Pasadena Rosebud Academy: 'Hey, I'm probably going to have to start my own school'

Shawn Brumfield was a banker who decided to become a teacher. When she became disenchanted with the way public schools were teaching young people, she decided to open her own school. Pasadena Rosebud Academy received its charter authorization in 2007. Since then, the school has become one of the most successful sites in

California, transforming the Achievement Gap into an opportunity for success.

The school is small, with only 178 students stretching from kindergarten through eighth grade. But the factors that fuel the Achievement Gap are present in every corner of the campus. Most Pasadena Rosebud students struggle with poverty, as 59 percent are eligible for free and reduced-price meals. The student body is almost entirely comprised of students of color – 64 percent are African American and 27 percent are Latino.

While such demographics typically predict the Achievement Gap, Pasadena Rosebud has created a far more positive narrative. In California standardized tests, 54 percent of the school's elementary students achieved proficiency in English Language Arts, with 47 percent proficient in mathematics. For the middle school grades, the numbers were similarly impressive: 62 percent were proficient in English and 41 percent in math. In every category, Pasadena Rosebud children performed better than the state average for all students. And those Pasadena kids far surpassed the California averages for African American children.

The success story begins with the founder. Brumfield completed her bachelor's degree in economics and began her professional career in the banking industry. After several years in finance, she began to think about changing paths. Teaching held a certain appeal. She took a year off, traveled to Spain and Mexico and learned to speak, read, and write in Spanish.

"I was just going to try teaching because I was open-minded and was open to different kinds of experiences," she said. "And thank goodness, because it turned out to be my passion and why I was put on this earth – to educate."

She began, as many professionals do while testing a new career, by hiring herself out as a substitute. Soon she was offered a full time teaching position at Woodrow Wilson Middle School in Pasadena, where she taught seventh and eighth grade English as a Second

Language courses. After several years, she moved to Los Angeles Unified and taught social studies. She loved teaching, but grew frustrated by the inadequate efforts she saw to help low-performing students of color improve their academic experiences. She had ideas for improvements, but understood she could not effect change in a large school bureaucracy. She recalled thinking, "Hey, I'm probably going to have to start my own school."

Brumfield knew something about administration from her banking days and work as a literacy coach and teacher trainer with the California Governor's Reading Institute. She began to study charter school rules in California and applied to Pasadena Unified for a charter to start Pasadena Rosebud. When the doors opened, 14 students arrived for classes in kindergarten and first grade. The school grew one grade level per year until it reached the eighth grade. Today it operates 175 days annually, with a bell schedule slightly longer than nearby traditional schools.

Given the founder's unusual path to success, it is not surprising to find several unique academic programs at Pasadena Rosebud. Brumfield created a financial literacy program for students, which is also designed to influence parents. Students set up bank accounts, learn about savings and interest, the stock market and other financial basics. The school partners with Junior Achievement USA to provide curriculum materials and speakers.

The principal's love of travel also became a cornerstone of the Pasadena Rosebud success story. Brumfield wants her students to realize the world extends far beyond the San Gabriel Valley. She encourages young people to develop broad cultural perspectives.

Each class takes a major field trip once a year. Eighth graders go to New York and Washington. Seventh graders visit Costa Rica. Sixth graders enroll at a marine science camp for three days. Fifth graders head to a mountain camp. The youngest children visit Southern California locations such as Legoland and Catalina Island. Every month, Pasadena Rosebud students go somewhere.

Traditional education strategies are not overlooked. Teachers focus on the California Common Core State Standards in most subjects. In English Language Arts, they emphasize reading comprehension, writing, listening, and speaking in complete sentences.

"Critical thinking is tied to these four language skills," Brumfield said. "Everything we do is designed to strengthen all four skills. Students take dictation to practice their spelling skills. So even at the kindergarten level, by the end of the year we want our students to have really strong paragraphs, introductory sentences, three supporting ideas, and a concluding sentence. Students are required to read every night, and we keep a reading log."

Pasadena Rosebud has a robust attitude toward tracking academic progress. The school is designed around small class sizes, with one class per grade level and class rosters in the low twenties. Teachers are given flexibility to group their students for instructional purposes, but data analysis assures that each student gets appropriate attention.

The school uses Achieve3000 – a computer program that helps monitor individual student progress. Teachers review benchmark tests produced by various publishers, including Prentice Hall, Pearson Education and Scott Foresman. When students complete a unit, they take a benchmark test. Performances are tracked before the benchmark test with chapter tests.

"As principal, I have high standards for everybody," Brumfield said. "I am passionate about teachers. I also push parent involvement. We believe in building positive relations with staff, parents and community. I insist upon consistency among teachers. We have key templates for lessons plans. We urge that teachers use academic vocabulary. We stress cross-curricular connection, which strengthens critical thinking."

Teaching at Pasadena Rosebud requires collaboration and teamwork. Brumfield hires educators who can philosophically accept that they are preparing students for careers and college. The principal insists that her staff have high expectations for themselves, their students, and parents.

"An important thing for me is building relationships," Brumfield said. "So building positive relationships with the staff, students, the parents, and the community has been huge for us. As we have a cooperative relationship, they don't want to let you down."

Professional development is offered the week before school starts. During the academic year, teachers dedicate one day per semester for professional development. The school's small size allows for easy and continual collaboration beyond the scheduled weekly staff meetings. Brumfield conducts teacher observations at the start of each year. She prepares an informal evaluation during the first semester and holds formal observations in the spring. Throughout the week, she roams the campus.

As noted, the partnership with parents is an important part of the school's strategy. Teachers send a weekly progress report home. Parents acknowledge the contents by their signatures. The Parent Teacher Organization meets bimonthly and briefs parents about how they can help their children at home. About 40 parents typically attend. The school provides incentives, with children receiving a treat the next day if their parents attend. "Later parents will say, 'My kids made me come,'" Brumfield said.

Parent-teacher conferences typically enjoy 100 percent participation at Pasadena Rosebud. If a parent misses one of the two annual conferences, the school follows up with a phone call.

With energy, persistence, passion and intelligence, Brumfield has built a remarkable experience on North Canon Boulevard in Altadena. The school's leadership has not changed since the first day of class in 2007. There is no Charter Management Organization, nor a traditional public school's bureaucracy. The school reflects one person's vision. Given the narrow operating scope, can the success of Pasadena Rosebud be duplicated elsewhere? The answer becomes obvious with a review of Brumfield's advice to colleagues.

She said, "Set high standards for everyone: your staff, your students, your parents, yourself. Build positive relationships with staff, parents and community. Push for parent involvement."

As for instructional leadership, she said, "You need consistency from grade level to grade level. We have some key components of lesson plans. We need to always use academic language and vocabulary with kids. Don't talk down to them. Every lesson should incorporate cross-curricular connections. Teachers should generate class discussions. Let students agree or disagree, but explain why."

Whether a school is large or small, rural, suburban or urban, Brumfield's advice is universal and readily transferable.

Public School 7:
'Set big goals for students and teachers'

Goals come in one size at Public School 7 in Sacramento – extra large. But unlike many schools, where goals are established for children but not necessarily the adults who teach them, PS 7 devotes considerable time, energy, and resources to coaching and developing its team of educators.

"There needs to be high expectations for teachers as well as students," said the school's principal, Kari Wehrly.

PS 7 – the name derives from the uniform number worn by the school's founder, Kevin Johnson, during his professional basketball career – serves students in kindergarten through eighth grade at two campuses in Sacramento. An elementary school guides children through the fifth grade. A middle school prepares students for high school. The middle school is located on the campus of Sacramento High School. Both sites are operated by the St. HOPE Charter Management Organization founded by Johnson, who served two terms as mayor of Sacramento. The schools are located in the Oak Park neighborhood where Johnson grew up.

Consistencies abound under the St. HOPE banner. Lesson plans are aligned among teachers by grade levels. Every student's progress and performance are continuously monitored. Classroom culture is considered an extremely important factor in student success at all St. HOPE schools. At the same time, parents are encouraged to make a personal investment in the academic experiences of their children, extending the classroom culture into every student's home life.

At PS 7, professional development is never far from any discussion. Teachers are nurtured and assisted by administrators and senior teaching coaches. Individual educators are seen as unique and essential components in the school's success, and never regarded as so many interchangeable parts.

One practice that every PS 7 teacher embraces involves "exit tickets." We have seen these devices used elsewhere in this chapter, and they produce effective results at diverse sites. Teachers ask students to submit their exit tickets at the end of each lesson. The tickets offer students an opportunity to explain what they learned from their instruction that day. Moreover, the tickets provide valuable feedback for the teacher and administrative team.

Teachers grade their student's exit tickets. The principal and teacher coaches meet with PS 7 educators weekly and review the student responses. The reviews help form the basis of planning sessions for the next round of instruction.

Another teaching practice at PS 7 is the use of the software program Illuminate to track student performance data, beginning in third grade. PS 7 administers benchmark tests once every quarter, and the resulting data is displayed and shared for English Language Arts, mathematics, and science for students in the fifth through eighth grades.

Administrative support for teachers is a constant and common theme at PS 7. Principal Wehrly described several practices that have become part of the school's culture. There is curriculum planning between administrators and teachers. The principal and her leadership team are available to meet with teachers most evenings and even weekends, if necessary.

PS 7 teachers receive 21 professional development days each year. The school calendar runs 175 days. Class periods last 85 minutes, which often allows for two lessons. The school day is rigorous. It starts at 7 a.m. and ends at 4 p.m.

When the bell strikes at 4 o'clock, the day may not be over. Teachers provide after-school interventions for students who need more help. Seventh grade has interventions in mathematics. Eighth graders are offered after-school tutorials. There are "reading blocks" for students who are not reading at their appropriate grade level. Small pullout sessions are available for reading help at each grade level.

Another component in the PS 7 strategy involves parents. The school takes multiple steps to make sure parents are consistently aware of the work being done by their children, Wehrly said. She described something called the Blue Communication Folders, which are sent home to parents. The Blue Folder contains a grade report and notes each child's mastery of standards. It communicates about office hours. Parents are asked to sign the Blue Folder, indicating they read it. Any parent or guardian can arrange for a consultation with their child's teacher as desired.

To comply with federal and state program requirements, PS 7 has a school Site Council. Special events such as "Whole Literacy Night" are attended by about 40 percent of the school's parents.

The emphasis on professional development and the building of relationships with parents has paid off at PS 7, both at the elementary and middle school levels.

The middle school students have performed slightly better than their younger peers in the PS 7 elementary grades on California standardized tests. PS 7 middle school students met English proficiency at 45 percent and reached mathematics proficiency at 40 percent. Both categorical scores exceeded the statewide average for African American students, and the PS 7 math scores were slightly above the statewide average for all students.

Wehrly acknowledged the elementary grades have become her key targets for improvement. Even so, the elementary grades at PS 7 outperformed statewide total for African American students in math.

Wehrly, a former Teach For America corps member in Hawaii, composed a list of four suggestions when asked how she would replicate the PS 7 model in other communities. Her focus on teachers was neither coincidental nor limited.

First, she would create a coaching structure for teachers. "Developing teachers is the key," she said. Second, she would insist that the curriculum reflect high expectations for students, while remaining appropriate for their age and grade levels. Third, she noted the word "investment," which she defined as, "Set big goals for students and teachers." Finally, she would focus on staffing. She said, "New hires need to know that we do whatever it takes to make the school excellent. Also, we avoid using outside substitute teachers. When someone is absent, we double up, because outsiders do not know our culture, and kids need consistency from day to day."

While Wehrly operates within the St. HOPE structure, the principal said she receives significant flexibility from the Charter Management Organization. With her world of relative autonomy and flexibility, she expressed satisfaction.

Sacramento High School:
'We want our kids to really be the best'

Success as a college preparatory institution is not enough for Sacramento High School. The historic campus, opened in 1924, is determined to move beyond the traditional yardstick of excellence — measured by impressive scores on standardized tests — and judge itself against the future.

Unlike many prep schools that consider their work finished when a student receives a diploma and heads off to college, Sacramento High wants its influence to stretch deep into the next chapter of education. It wants that influence to be measurable. The school is trying to make sure its young people are admitted to four-year colleges or universities – and handle the transition to adulthood, manage independence and earn college degrees.

"My leadership tenure will focus on how we go from being a really good school, in a lot of ways, versus actually achieving our mission of having our kids graduate from a four-year college or university," said Shannon Wheatley, who was appointed principal at Sacramento High in 2017. "Beyond tracking how we perform on the state test, I think there are really two tests that matter because they are in direct line to our mission. These are the ACT and SAT. We know that kids have to take the ACT and the SAT to get into college. So part of what we want to do is align toward those assessments. The data we get from ACT is rich, and it is something that we can use to make actionable changes for classroom teachers."

Wheatley, formerly a site leader and school founder with the KIPP charter system in Houston, is running one of the most ambitious and successful programs of its kind in California. Operated by the St. HOPE public Charter Management Organization since 2003, Sacramento High has consistently closed the Achievement Gap.

The school's ability to help guide its students into college is extraordinary, with about 95 percent of Sacramento High graduates moving directly into higher education. Approximately 65 percent are admitted to four-year universities, while the rest prepare during two years at community colleges. The numbers are remarkable for a school in an economically disadvantaged, slowly gentrifying neighborhood with 69 percent of its students eligible for free or reduced meal plans.

In 2017, Sacramento High enrolled 902 students, including 61 percent African American and 24 percent Latino. Those students exceeded statewide averages on the California assessment tests. Sacramento High students scored 65 percent proficient in English Language Arts and 24 percent proficient in math. Statewide averages for African Americans are 31 percent in ELA and 19 percent in math.

Sacramento High was the only California high school in 2017 with greater than 50 percent African American enrollment to attain scores above statewide averages for African Americans in both English and math. The school scored higher percentages in English than the averages for all students statewide.

Wheatley gives credit to his educators — "It's always the teachers," he said — but the high scores and enviable college acceptance rates transcend individual staff members and principals. Success at Sacramento High is the result of a strategic, goal-oriented approach to learning, plus a systematic support system for students, their families and teachers. The teachers and campus leaders become part of the system, cogs in the wheel, which relies on professional buy-in, data reviews and collegiality and leaves very little to chance.

Sacramento High has 37 teaching positions. Each person hired for those jobs is welcomed into an environment that provides several shoulders to lean upon. The support is direct and consistent. Every teacher is assigned a coach. At the beginning of the relationship, coaches spend significant time in the classroom. Planning conferences are scheduled between the educator and coach, and observations and debriefings occur at least once over a two-week period. The coaches include department chairs, grade-level chairs, two assistant principals and the school's vice-principal, Jim Scheible, a St. HOPE veteran. Scheible is also responsible for operations and discipline at Sacramento High.

"Our teachers know we want to be more standards based," Scheible said. "That includes college readiness standards, next-generation science standards, and the standards in the Advanced Placement classes."

The administrators realize not every teacher arrives with the same skills and experiences. Some will need more help than others — "intervention" is the word used by Sacramento High. Explained Scheible, "We want to get to a place where we can take any teacher and grow them from where they are, to improved academic performance, behavior, attendance and effort from their students."

Principal Wheatley also visits classrooms, typically for 10 to 20 minutes. He has established a protocol for all of his professional observers, so teachers and coaches know what to expect from each other. For openers, they want to see visible lesson plans and a lesson objective on the board. They want to see rigorous objectives that match what the students are actually working on.

More subjectively, observers seek to measure the classroom culture. They look for urgency and even joy in students. They want to see whether the teacher monitors the class for understanding, and whether students follow their teacher's guidelines. Finally, they want to see progress from previous observations.

Sacramento High administrators understand that teachers can only be as good as their leadership. Educators cannot be expected to become visionary instructors without support from their bosses. "You have to set a clear vision," Wheatley said. "And you have got to have teachers that align that vision and the systems needed to support that vision."

The cornerstone of the vision is the acknowledgement that Sacramento High students present themselves each day with a diverse and unique set of needs. Wheatley said, "Teaching with this demographic requires that you work differently and harder than anywhere else. Teachers and staff need to be able to confront and push kids to see themselves as better than what society is currently telling them that they can accomplish."

The ultimate accomplishment for Sacramento High students is graduation from college. The school has built a mission around making its young people understand they can manage college-level academic rigors and are worthy of university admission. The goal of going to college drives instruction, intervention and support. It's infused into the Sacramento High culture.

"The use of your time and your money should demonstrate that getting kids to be able to graduate from college is your top priority," Wheatley said. "We want our kids to really be the best, because the world they are going to face is just so complex. The real thing is, I want to provide the counter-narrative to the Black educational experiences here in Sacramento."

The work comes alive in the classrooms. Third-year English teacher Kimanh Truong-Munoz, oversees one such room. Munoz directs the Advance Placement and Honors courses in her subject area. A primary focus for her is the students' growth in reading and writing — growth tracked as data. If college success is the ultimate mission at Sacramento High, data is the fuel for attainment. Practically everything a Sacramento High student does is charted and entered into a database for review, comparison, and measurement.

As part of its drive to build and sustain success by marshaling the power of data, Sacramento High classes include regular assessments, both informal and formative. The AP and Honors English courses under Munoz are no exception. At the start of the year, her students take reading and vocabulary tests. They repeat the process quarterly, with progress tracked and assessed. The tests come from item banks produced by Scholastic Reading Inventory and Illuminate Assessments, which are designed to align with the Common Core Standards that appear on California's annual standardized tests.

Munoz has expressed reservations about strictly teaching to the state assessments. She said she and her fellow English teachers have developed independent ways to create benchmarks against which to measure student progress. She modifies instruction based on those independent assessments. Moreover, she deploys teacher-created tests, especially when she wants to measure progress in writing, which she said she measures "a lot."

Another strategy in Munoz' classroom is the use of "exit tickets," where students produce short responses to questions designed to establish whether the student has mastered the day's lesson. From these protocols came a 65 percent proficiency rate in ELA on state tests for 2017 — a number that held for all Sacramento High students, including African Americans.

Teachers are encouraged to support each other with a scheduling device called "common preparation period," which allows educators from the same subject area to meet and share the progress of their students, along with any corrective actions. The school schedules monthly grade-level team meetings, where staff members discuss successful practices. The meetings encourage teachers to seek help and engagement from their peers.

"When I first started here (under a different principal), I never saw another adult the entire day," one teacher said. "We were in our own little silos and never talked to anyone else about our students. The most beneficial professional development occurs when you come together and there is an agenda, objectives and a common goal that is student-centered. People walk away feeling as if it was purposeful."

Collegiality and data may be essential to administrators and educators at Sacramento High, but they don't directly inspire students to believe they can compete with their suburban, college-bound peers. Inspiration requires a human touch. U.S. History

AP and Honors teacher Amy Bostick begins her academic year with positive lessons in self-reliance.

"I've learned over the years with my population that I have to build confidence," she said. "They are getting messages that they are not good enough. I have to convince my kids that you can do this! And it gets results. It's just working on their psyches."

Bostick starts with a student self-evaluation early in the year. Then she moves into one-on-one sessions — "I don't assume anything," she said. The strategies came from investigative work in the field. Bostick visited schools where 100 percent of the students passed AP exams. She noted their classroom practices. She also became an AP expert, serving as an official grader for the exam, networking with other graders and enrolling in training courses. The teacher sought to reverse roles by taking the AP U.S. History exam under the same time limits and conditions that confronted her students.

Structurally, the Social Studies Department at Sacramento High is vertically aligned, which means teachers in each grade agree on the range of topics taught at that level. Under the arrangement, ninth-grade curriculum continues to a specific point, which yields to 10th grade curriculum, and so on. Nothing is taken for granted. Said Bostick, "Kids have problems with reading, literacy and inference. So we build our programs to teach those things."

Sacramento High students face multiple challenges, but many challenges are predictable. For example, some of the young people have minimal keyboard skills. Teachers admit to sadness while watching students painstakingly type out papers in the computer lab.

Another problematic area concerns teachers themselves. Retention has been a consistent burden for the campus. When the retention challenge is multiplied across a student's entire primary and secondary educational experience, it becomes apparent why many students fall behind early in their academic careers and arrive at high school less than fully prepared.

David Marks, a Sacramento High college counselor, said, "The biggest obstacle our students face is lack of access to highly qualified teachers throughout their K-12 experience. Attracting and keeping excellent, qualified educators is a big problem. The teacher determines so much of how much a student can achieve."

Marks has seen Sacramento High lose teachers to suburban districts because the suburbs can make an educator's professional life easier, if less satisfying. Marks said, "Another struggle we face is just plain literacy, including mathematical literacy. Our students are so frequently pushed from one grade to the next in elementary and middle school without becoming effective readers and gleaners of information from text. Even our AP students, we have to teach a lot of literacy, and these are our top students."

Despite the challenges, Marks pointed to the work of teachers such as Munoz and Bostick as he noted the school sent nine seniors to UC Irvine and seven to UCLA in 2017, the best numbers in Sacramento High memory.

The drive to get students admitted to highly selective universities is a methodical, supportive process for every professional working at Sacramento High. Students are tracked through the year on progress and milestones. Each fall, Counselor Marks meets with every senior. He described the meetings as crucial: they allow him to build trusting relationships with individual students. "If they are eligible for something, I make sure they apply for it. I really want them to be successful."

The trust is formed in the junior year, when the counselor meets students in groups. For third-year students, he reviews grades, transcripts and standardized test scores. He examines the list of college applications that each student plans to complete. He ensures the plans align with reality.

"Discussions with students individually is critical because there are two camps: ones who think that they can do anything and go anywhere, including the best universities in the world, even though their records may be sub-average," Marks said. "The other group — the vast majority — thinks, 'College is not my environment. No one I know has gone there. It seems very white or Asian. It's no place I'm comfortable with.' It's part of my work to help them to be more optimistic about themselves."

The alignment of standardized test scores with a student's university admission prospects is an essential part of the Sacramento High experience. The school uses Measurement of Academic Progress (MAP) tests correlated with the ACT exam to predict performances on standardized assessments. Eventually, Principal Wheatley expects to use ACT data to predict how students will perform in their first year of college. "Our North Star is in that direction," he said.

A final component of Sacramento High's success has nothing to do with data. The school nurtures relationships with parents and guardians, believing support must continue when the student leaves campus and heads for home. Academic intervention conferences are called when a student is failing two or more classes at any midterm or interim break. Parents, teachers and student are brought together to create an action plan with follow-up steps. If behavior is behind the problem, special contracts are written for the student, with expectations spelled out.

"These parent conference are very important," Wheatley said. "We try to present to the student and to the family a picture of a body of their work so that we can have a grown-up conversation. We say to the student, 'This is where you are on paper. Is this where you want to be?'"

The interventions have substantially reduced suspensions, approximately by 50 percent. Wheatley credited the interventions for "being really clear on expectations and coaching people and holding them accountable."

Sacramento High parents are encouraged to visit school. They are constantly being told the doors are open for them. They receive weekly grade books. And when parents can't come to school, teachers can arrange home visits, a strategy Wheatley plans to expand. Teachers are encouraged to maintain regular lines of communication, quarterly if not monthly. Said Munoz, "It's our responsibility to get parents to attend meetings, and it is on us if they are not there."

Parents can also communicate through technology. The school uses the software platform Illuminate Student Information, and parents can log on and check their student's progress. Sacramento High uses Chromebook laptops to familiarize students with the devices they will use for the state standardized tests. The leadership concedes that access to computers has been a shortcoming at Sacramento High. The school has three computer labs, but only seniors have unlimited access. Other students must sometimes wait in line.

Despite its shortage of computers, Sacramento High has built a formidable reputation for success in overcoming the Achievement Gap. Several teachers were asked how they would replicate the school's experiences at another school. One teacher said, "A student will not learn from you if they don't respect you and believe in you. So you must have a culture of success." The teacher also cited professional team building among educators in each subject area, and becoming expert in the tests taken by students.

Another educator emphasized the importance of high expectations, including graduation requirements that exceed the "A to G" requirements used by the University of California and California State University systems. Among the requirements at Sacramento High is a community service component. One teacher noted the longer days — the Sacramento High bell schedule runs from 7:55 a.m. to 3:35 p.m., longer than traditional schools in the Sacramento area. Class periods are 75 minutes.

"Sacramento High School has sent a high number of first-generation, low-income Latino and African American student to college in the past few years, and we are going to continue that mission," Wheatley said. "We are focused on continuing to provide a robust high school experience that is still personalized in a way that kids feel a connection to the school. They have access to adults who love them, and who are here for them."

Watts Learning Center:
'A dynamic place to learn and work'

The first day of school was not impressive. There were three teachers, one office manager and a principal. Classrooms were organized inside a weary bungalow shared with a Head Start preschool program at Hacienda Village, a bleak South Los Angeles housing project.

Hacienda Village spilled across six blocks on Compton Avenue. It was a brisk walk from two other sprawling projects, Nickerson Gardens and Jordan Downs, built in Watts soon after World War II, communities designed with government contracts and architectural schemes reminiscent of cellblocks. Educational opportunities — or opportunities of any kind — were dismal in this corner of Los Angeles. The streets were notorious for other reasons. They were prodigious recruiting grounds for gangs.

Hundreds of young men from Hacienda and Nickerson and the Jordan projects pledged their allegiance — and lives — to the Bounty Hunter Bloods, Circle City Piru, Hacienda Village Bloods and Grape Street Crips. Gangs terrorized the housing projects. They killed and wounded bystanders, sold drugs, and murdered each other.

Only two students from the community, both kindergarteners too young and innocent for gangs, presented themselves for class on that first day of school at Hacienda Village, September 9, 1997. The other seats were empty. But those two children represented a victory. They were pioneers in a new civic movement for quality education, the first young people to step forward and join an ambitious school built from nothing called the Watts Learning Center.

Twenty years after that tentative first day, Watts Learning Center has become one of a handful of California schools to successfully attack, narrow and fill the Achievement Gap. With two sites serving elementary and middle school youngsters and a new $9 million expansion opened in 2017, Watts Learning Center serves a student population that defines the Achievement Gap with all its anguish, frustration, potential, hope, and opportunity.

The school is 50 percent African American and 47 percent Latino. Ninety-five percent of the children are eligible for free and reduced meals. Within those student cohorts, the performance data has been consistent and impressive for Watts Learning Center. The results can be measured over many years under diverse assessment methods.

Graded by the Academic Performance Index, which California used from 1999 through 2013, Watts Learning Center exceeded the state's mandated goals four years in a row, with scores above 800. When California remodeled its standards and established Common Core, Watts Learning Center slipped slightly, but still performed significantly above average for students who struggle with the Achievement Gap.

In 2017, the school's elementary students met or exceeded proficiency in English Language Arts at a rate of 43 percent — slightly below the statewide overall average of 49 percent but well above the state average for African American students at 31 percent.

The story was even better in 2017 statewide, standardized assessments for math, where Watts Learning Center elementary students met or exceeded proficiency at 44 percent. The statewide overall average was 38 percent. Statewide, African Americans scored 19 percent in math.

The results produced by Watts Learning Center are not unique to South Los Angeles. The results have not evolved from experimental curriculums or revolutionary instructional methods. Similar outcomes can be obtained by any school that is willing to work hard and adopt certain basic principles — to establish a flexible array of time-proven protocols and management systems, mixed with the timeless attributes of collaboration, respect and accountability.

"The success of our school community depends upon the collaboration, commitment and involvement of parents, students, teachers and community members," Kelly Baptiste, Watts Learning Center director, said. "We know that our families are an essential part of our school community, as they are our children's first teachers. We believe they are our most valuable resource in helping our students to succeed. We know that collaborative decision making with strong staff and parent involvement makes our school a dynamic place to learn and work."

In June 1997, Watts Learning Center, known by its initials, WLC, became one of the first inner-city schools granted a charter by the Los Angeles Unified School District. The charter concept was relatively new in California in 1997. While WLC had prodigious support — the School Futures Research Foundation offered the school $100,000 a year in startup costs — the early days were difficult.

Surveying the empty seats in the bungalow at Hacienda Village, WLC organizers quickly realized they needed a new school site. They talked with residents from the community and learned many parents were supportive and interested in the idea of a new school, but were afraid to send their children into a housing project overrun by gangs.

A search for a new site began almost immediately. Within 18 months, Watts Learning Center had moved several blocks northwest, into a former Catholic girls school on Manchester Avenue. By then, the school had two grades, kindergarten and first. Enrollment was 120 students.

Despite the foundational dollars, challenges continued. Money was never abundant. The founders had to chase financial support, leveraging business contacts and friendships. But the leaders were motivated and resourceful, and not the sort of people who easily gave up. And while they were devoted to improving the educational opportunities for South Los Angeles children, they were for the most part not professional educators. Most were business executives and professionals who were inspired by a sense of collective dismay over the quality of public education available to young people in Watts.

"It started with the fact that we were not happy with the performance of the children in our community," Eugene Fisher said. A former government consultant, Fisher became president of the WLC board of directors and served as the school's Chief Executive Officer.

The motivation to improve student performance has driven WLC for 20 years. As the school celebrated its 20th anniversary in 2017, the legacy of empty desks filling a bungalow in a dangerous housing project served as an image from a distant past.

The school moved into a renovated, 12,500 foot building in 2008, and opened a separate middle school for sixth, seven and eight grades the next year. The middle school grades eventually moved to classrooms at a newer Los Angeles Unified high school, Mervyn Dymally, about 12 blocks from the WCL elementary campus. In 2017, WLC enrollment was 397 for the middle school, and 367 for the elementary campus. For our purposes in this chapter, the focus and data are on the elementary school. The middle school had not yet duplicated the success found at the elementary level.

The success of Watts Learning Center is very much a story of teamwork and clearly defined and unified goals. Across two decades, three distinct components — teachers, families, and administrators — have contributed to the program's remarkable student outcomes. Each component brings a unique perspective. Each serves students with equal significance. None could have succeeded alone.

A distinct pattern emerged when WLC teachers were asked how they might advise colleagues from other schools. The educators didn't mention English Language Arts or math test scores. Rather, they focused on systemic strategies and humanistic approaches.

"Teachers need a great management system where routines are taught, especially in the first month of school," said Cynthia Clark, a teacher who handles both fourth and fifth grades. "You communicate a rewards system for students who perform well."

Kameron O'Daniel, a fourth-grade teacher, focuses on rules and structure. He said, "You must establish a culture of respect and accountability, creating consequences for behavior and accomplishments as found in the real world. I teach to the high end. It benefits the low- and middle-achieving students. Then I address them in small groups."

Conflict resolution became an important tool in building successful habits at WLC. Appropriate resolution skills were emphasized early in the classroom of third grade teacher Sima Aleahmad, who believes in setting and resetting the proper tone for learning. "I create a Circle of Love, where once a week for about 25 minutes, we address conflict resolution by having students say what they like or do not like about the classroom," Aleahmad said.

Administrative support is one of several regimens built into WLC protocols. Teachers value the Friday grade-level meetings, which help inspire collaboration among the staff. Educators appreciate how management encourages them to attend conferences and pursue professional development. Administrators maintain an open door, and solicit input from staff. The school provides an environment for stable employment, and younger, newer teachers don't fear the layoff notices that accompany annual budget shortfalls at many traditional public schools. Another benefit is modest but important: each teacher receives a $250 annual stipend for classroom supplies.

"Teachers need to have time to adequately plan collaboratively," said school director Baptiste. "Teachers have to teach students how to read information, form an opinion, and write or speak about it coherently."

At Watts Learning Center, the result is a demonstrably light-hearted, secure and happy team of educators. One teacher said,

"When you have happy teachers who are happy to come to work, because of the environment created by the administrators and the founders, then, hey, it trickles down to the students."

As noted, the WLC founders were generally not professional educators. But they were professional administrators and business and community leaders. They understood management. And they recognized the need for experienced leadership at the school site administrative level.

Sandra Porter, a retired principal for Los Angeles Unified, joined the founders and became one of the first professional educators recruited to help run the school. Twenty years later, she remained a consistent and familiar presence on campus, giving and receiving hugs from dozens of students as she walked the grounds. Her commitment to Watts Learning Center was underscored by her marriage to Gene Fisher, the CEO.

As new administrators and staff moved through the school, a philosophy was created to transcend individual personalities and serve as inspiration for the program. The founders settled on four guideline statements. Significantly, the guidelines are focused on children. Only the final statement makes any reference to adults:

1. Every child must be known, understood and respected because children are at the center of the educational process.

2. Children play an active role in the learning process.

3. Educational experiences should enable students to communicate effectively, solve problems competently, think critically and creatively, and act responsibly.

4. Parent involvement and volunteer services support and enhance the teaching and learning process.

Collaboration among students, parents, staff, administrators and community members stands at the heart of the Watts Learning

Center philosophy. Collaboration is on display across the school, and extends to programs designed to broaden the horizons of children who may not have traveled far beyond Watts. The school organizes annual trips to the wilderness of Lake Hughes in the Angeles National Forest north of Los Angeles. Other journeys have transported students much greater distances. Classes have visited Senegal, South Africa, Togo, Egypt, and Brazil.

Back home, each student has a personal email account and access to a computer. Every book in the WLC curriculum is available on line. Students write papers on Google document software, which allows teachers to provide quick and clear feedback. Baptiste, the school director, does not require daily lesson plans from her 16 teachers. Rather, she receives "units of study" every six weeks from teacher groups across all grade levels.

Student progress is tracked by Grade Pro software, which lets teachers and administrators efficiently monitor individual student progress and modify instruction as needed. For math studies, the school uses the innovative Singapore program, which focuses on a three-step learning process — concrete, pictorial and abstract — and allows students to master fewer math concepts in greater detail.

"School leaders must get buy-in with the expectations for school culture, the use of data-driven instruction and the use of feedback on how and what to improve based upon administrators' observations," Baptiste said

The collaborative spirit is visible in every classroom. Administrators stop by for daily visits. Early releases are granted to teachers for professional development every Wednesday, plus one Friday each month. Teacher recruitment, often a problem in urban school environments, has been mitigated with a collaboration that stretches to the shores of the Great Lakes. WLC has tapped a wellspring of new educators by building a teacher training and placement program with Hope College, a Christian school in Holland, Michigan.

The third component to collaboration at Watts Learning Center involves parents and family members. Family relationships can be complex, and the staff and administration acknowledge that some WLC students face chaotic environments at home.

One veteran teacher has noticed a cultural shift in recent years, with fewer grandparents and aunts or uncles stepping forward to help raise children whose parents worked multiple jobs. The teacher said single parents seem have more difficultly finding backup support from family members, a dilemma which increases the challenges for the children.

Help can be found on campus, from a squad of "foster grandparents" who provide a calming and restorative presence. Trained in a program administrated by Pepperdine University, the grandparents are intervention specialists. They can pull a troubled student aside or temporarily escort a student from a classroom. They are trained to calm the youngster and prevent trouble from escalating. They frequently reduce or eliminate the need for disciplinary action, and allow other students to stay on task. The grandparents also assist with classroom chores. Not surprisingly, they are beloved by teachers and students.

Fortunately, a majority of Watts Learning Center students have parents or responsible adults who can monitor classroom progress and communicate with the school. One father told his daughter's teacher that math was an exceedingly difficult subject for the youngster. The teacher obtained audio lessons for the father to review together with his daughter at home. After several weeks of the home reviews, the girl began to excel in math.

Another parent spoke with a third-grade teacher about a struggling student. The teacher provided instructional materials to take home, and the parent established a consistent practice of reviewing her daughter's homework for two hours daily. The intervention worked. The mother said, "When my daughter goes back to school, she is right on point with the rest of her class."

Watts Learning Center asks parents to volunteer 25 hours each semester. Though volunteer service is not mandatory, many parents appreciate the opportunity to become part of the educational process. One parent said, "I think it helps the child do better in school. Our teacher encourages us to read to the child every day. She says, 'Have your child read to you on the way to school.' On Saturdays she suggested that we go to the library and help her pick out books she may enjoy. All of this helps my daughter and encourages her to want to do better in school."

Other parents find ways to extend the learning process at home. A mother uses flash cards to help her third-grader with sight words. "We look up the words and write short sentences on what the sight words mean," the parent said. "We also use flash cards with math: multiplication facts. I recognize that it is more than the required homework, so I reward her with things she likes — movies, places she likes to go, little extras."

With its emphasis on collaboration, Watts Learning Center has helped to build and nurture buy-in and partnerships with parents. Parents and family members provide support, and they extend the teaching process when their children are at home and away from the classroom. Parents receive weekly report cards and are encouraged to give rewards and consequences to their children. Parents are also encouraged to bring any concerns directly to the teacher, without bringing children into the discussion.

"My son has been here since kindergarten," one parent said. "Throughout that time, the teachers have shown him how to take notes. I am able to look at his notes daily and see what he did, and what he needs to do. We always encouraged our children to read, at least 45 minutes, different books. He chooses books that will excite him."

Another parent described the communication network between teacher and parent — an essential tool for monitoring progress. "We exchange emails with my daughter's teacher. We text.

They send notes and reports every day, but I'm not always able to call her back. So I think our role is to encourage our kids, support the teacher and the staff because most of the time they are with the child more than we are. We can't just leave it all on the teachers and staff to teach our kids. We have to do our parts, too."

Baptiste succinctly explained WLC expectations for the relationship between educators and parents: "Teachers must value working with the families of their students."

School CEO Gene Fisher is often asked to give advice to parents, administrators, and educators eager to duplicate the success of Watts Learning Center. His playbook is grounded in self-reflection, honesty and the realization that schools must be holistic community enterprises, built on cornerstones of civic agreement and acceptance.

"Be grounded in why you want to start a school," he said. "Then reach out to your perspective community and find out what they want. We found out early that our parents want a safe school. They want service like daycare when there are required meetings or other events for adults. They want food for the children — three times a day. Then, they were ready to listen to us talk about quality education."

The community must believe a school can improve conditions in the neighborhood, Fisher said. He listed "mutual respect" as one core value that must be embraced by all factions. And leadership must be stable.

"Once you are clear about the goals, you need to find a quality staff," Fisher said. "Then you need to involve your community to make sure that they will support your plan of operation, like a 7 a.m. start time and a 6 p.m. closing time, if necessary."

Educating young people is never an easy or carefree task, and it is inherently difficult in a gritty, economically disadvantaged and underserved environment such as Watts. But with community partnerships, collaboration that extends from parents to staff and administration, and boundless respect for the common goal of adults educating children, Watts Learning Center has proved the job of closing the Achievement Gap is inherently possible.

Wilder's Preparatory Academy: 'High expectations for everything'

Excellence is the daily standard at Wilder's Preparatory Academy Charter School on North La Brea Avenue in Inglewood. But while excellence is expected and almost routine at Wilder, it is also systemic. It is built into the fabric of the school and never left to chance.

This strategic approach to excellence is demonstrated by a decision to devote significant resources — eight full time positions — to a cadre of professional educators called "intervention specialists." There is one specialist for each grade level and two subject areas, English Language Arts and math. Remarkable outcomes have followed, placing Wilder among the most successful schools in California with a majority African American student population.

The Wilder intervention specialists travel a path worn smooth by success. Their protocols unfold with the calendar. Six weeks into each new school year, every specialist receives a caseload filled with students whose progress has been weighed down by academic frustrations. The specialists develop a unique focus for each student in the caseload.

Help is provided with lessons designed to overcome whatever the academic challenge may be. Once the students have improved their study habits, outlook, retention or other concerns under the specialist's tutelage, the young scholars return to their regular classroom instruction. They are confident, refreshed and productive. At Wilder, intervention specialists are available throughout the year to help any student who needs a little extra guidance.

When two seventh-grade Wilder students were asked to discuss the features that make their school successful, they quickly mentioned those eight intervention specialists. One student explained how the specialists help untangle eternally frustrating academic challenges — such as how to determine percentages. As the lessons take root and percentages become a baseline skill, the student can resume his algebra assignments, refine the computations, and succeed.

The strategy that created the intervention specialist fits within an alliterative descriptor called the "Wilder Way." The philosophy dates from 1983, when a husband and wife team, Raymond and Carolyn Wilder, opened a pre-school called Tender Care Child Development Center. The school eventually grew to 180 students, ages two to five. The children were introduced to a curriculum-based approach to learning, along with appropriate opportunities for play and fun. By 1999, Tender Care had been renamed Wilder's Preparatory Academy. Class-level offerings expanded to include kindergarten through eighth grade.

The success has been consistent and worthy of study and replication. Wilder has obliterated the Achievement Gap. Consider the numbers: Wilder's enrollment is about 82 percent African American and 16 percent Latino. Seventy-seven percent of Wilder's students are economically disadvantaged and qualify for free or reduced-price meals. Yet both Wilder schools — elementary and middle — produced results on the 2017 standardized California tests that far exceed statewide averages for all demographic groups.

Wilder proficiency in English Language Arts was 69 percent for the school's elementary children and 74 percent for the middle school. The statewide overall average was 49 percent, with African American youngsters scoring 31 percent across California.

For math, the outcomes were similar in 2017. Wilder elementary students were proficient at a 61 percent rate. The Wilder middle school reached 44 percent proficiency. Statewide overall averages were 31 percent for all demographic groups, and 19 percent for African Americans.

Like several other successful school founders profiled in this edition, Raymond and Carolyn Wilder did not follow an obvious or direct course into primary and secondary-level educational leadership. They did other work first, and found their calling in middle age. Raymond, who died in 2013, worked in business management and ran several companies. His entrepreneurial spirit carried him from the wholesale seafood trade to real estate development. Carolyn was a professor of child development at West Los Angeles College, a community college in Culver City.

Despite their diverse professional backgrounds, the motivation to educate children ran deep within the Wilders. As Raymond Wilder explained to me in 2010, "I was inspired to get involved in education by my great-great grandfather — a slave — who taught people to read in a church and school he built in Arkansas."

Raymond directed me to a picture of that inspirational school, an image on display in the foyer of Wilder's Preparatory Academy today. The legacy continues despite Raymond's passing. Carolyn Wilder and daughter Ramona Wilder are fixtures at the campus. Ramona serves as the school's Chief Executive Officer, and Carolyn is a constant presence at the institution she founded with her husband.

Two key employees are responsible for operational leadership at Wilder's Prep: Germaine Jackson, the school's principal, and Rosalyn Robinson, assistant principal.

The school is organized within a 37,000 square foot building that includes 22 classrooms, library, gym, cafeteria, and labs. The elementary and middle schools are co-located within the Wilder facility, but are run on separate bell schedules. As principal, Jackson is responsible for both schools. Enrollment was 379 for the elementary school, and 188 for the middle school in 2017.

While the eight intervention specialists have been essential to Wilder's success in bridging and soaring beyond the Achievement

Gap, they are not the only reasons for the school's exceptional outcomes. Jackson, Wilder's principal, describes an environment where every effort is made to ensure students are well prepared for college and can demonstrate their proficiencies on the state's standardized tests.

A delegation of Wilder's teachers was sent to training conducted by the California Department of Education, where the educators learned the nuances of Common Core testing, with emphasis on English Language Arts. The teachers returned to Inglewood and taught their colleagues the lessons they had mastered. Test preparation strategies are woven into professional development, using a method called the Wilder's Model for Excellence in English Language Arts and Literacy.

Every Wilder's teacher attended a Common Core Interim Assessment Hand Scoring workshop and Digital Library training session. Administrators participated in other Common Core events. The professional development focus and emphasis on California's system of standardized testing created a facility well prepared to instruct within the rigors of Common Core.

Wilder's teachers used backwards planning, starting with the skill sets students would need to succeed on interim tests. The Wilder's team used digital library platforms to access lessons across the curriculum, which ensured that relevant materials were vetted and arranged to enhance unit and lesson plans.

"We have high expectations for everything that happens here," Jackson said. "It applies to students, staff and parents. We hold traditional values. It is expected that students do their homework, that teachers are prepared, that teachers are role models. We expect teachers to have passion, constantly. We expect parents to be involved."

The "Wilder Way" celebrates the need for everyone — students, parents, teachers and staff — to contribute to the school's success. But the Wilder method clearly believes the single most influential person to stimulate a young person's scholarly ambitions is the professional educator. Robinson, the assistant principal, said, "We want our expectations to be known. Teachers have to help with that. We tell teachers they must want to be here. They must help create a system with strong families."

Motivation comes from Wilder's culture of excellence, not exceptional monetary rewards. The average salary for a Wilder teacher is $46,000, with the most senior educators earning in the low $50,000 range. The salaries are slightly below the rates paid by the surrounding Inglewood Unified School District.

But Wilder's teachers form bonds and make commitments. There are few job openings at the school, and many of the educators have been on staff for at least seven years. Those teachers report each day to a job that rewards innovation and professional development, and that honors student success.

Wilder operates with a block schedule, which allows students to spend two full instructional periods immersed in the materials and learning targets. Teachers were given time to plan discussion and writing lessons, to receive feedback, and take deep dives into the texts and instructional material.

An important tool at Wilder is the Smarter Balanced system, which allows fair and meaningful assessments to help support students with learning difficulties. As students and teachers become fluent on the Smarter Balanced portal, they focus on the content of the assessment, not the technological features.

Technology plays multiple roles at Wilder. Software allows teachers to record and report student progress. Several educators use Adopted Mind, a program that assists with word problems for math, and Study Island, a practice tool that tracks student progress and allows for easy assessment and monitoring.

But the embrace of technology and a culture of high expectations do not completely explain Wilder's remarkable success. In some cases, the explanation is found in the traditional place — a teacher's skill, intuition and sensitivity. Part of that explanation involves the educator's interaction with students as determined by class size. Wilder elementary classes have no more than 22 students. For middle school, the number is 25. Those class sizes are smaller than most inner-city public schools.

Blessed with smaller classes, educators have the flexibility to maneuver, especially with struggling students. Mary Clemons, a third-grade teacher, says the needs of low-performing students are met with unique approaches. Sometimes, a high performer is paired with a struggling peer. Other times, students are divided into smaller groups with similar needs.

Kimberly Padgett-Willis, who teaches seventh and eight grade English Language Arts, makes frequent writing assignments, where students learn to produce quick and coherent mini-essays. Her top performers create PowerPoint presentations and share special reports with classmates.

Aside from her belief in the benefits of writing early and often, Padgett-Willis is a strong advocate for technology's role in the instructional game plan. "Technology is critical," she said. Her students prepare documents on computers and email the material to their teacher. They create videos with Apple iMovie, and use Google Scholar, a search engine for scholarly literature.

The Wilder administration supports instructional uses for technology and appreciates an innovative teacher. From staff to administrators, the Wilder team follows a philosophy of mutual aid, where everyone pulls together. Said Padgett-Willis, "I find it helpful to have administrators I can relate to."

From classroom to classroom, the bonds between Wilder's students and adult professionals play out in subtle ways. Student discussions are spirited, and teachers use creative games to push academic content. One teacher uses a math version of the game "Jeopardy." Consistencies abound. Classroom bulletin boards are uniformly neat, creative and inspiring. Rules, lesson objectives and assignments are on prominent display. Every student at Wilder wears a uniform, though the styles are distinct for both the elementary and middle schools.

The final element in the Wilder Way recipe for excellence is the parent. While the school takes its professional responsibilities very seriously, it recognizes that even the most successful strategies will fail without cooperation from parents.

Each Wilder's parent is asked to provide 40 hours of volunteer service every year. Parents are requested to consider and support a list of school expectations, which help transform student success into a shared responsibility between Wilder's professionals and the children's parents or guardians.

Among the expectations for parents are to support the uniform policy, adhere to standards of behavior at school, monitor their student's efforts at home study, collaborate with teachers and attend scheduled conferences and meetings, and support Wilder's special programs and activities. Some parents are asked to attend a class or two and observe their student.

There is no hesitation about getting parents involved. Padgett-Willis has been known to call parents at work in the middle of the day to address problems requiring immediate attention. When a parent sits in a classroom, the added adult presence and show of support often makes for a fast improvement in student behavior.

Mary Clemons, the third-grade teacher, estimates 98 percent of the parents in her class respond favorably to a meeting request. She may be more fortunate than some of her colleagues, but Clemons believes 90-85 percent of Wilder's parents will attend a meeting when asked by a teacher.

Wilder's success is well known across South Los Angeles and nearby communities such as Inglewood. Some parents travel many miles each day to deliver their children to North La Brea Avenue and bring them home after class. They believe the reward is worth the sacrifice in commute time, gasoline and anxiety.

The data and test results support the wisdom of those parental choices, and have been consistent for many years. If the search for solutions to the Achievement Gap could be reduced to just one location, Wilder's Prep in Inglewood would be a good place to start.

Two

The Research:
Recognizing what works

The Second Edition of *Bridging the Achievement Gap* is a story about excellent schools. Given the continued bleak news about the Achievement Gap and how it impacts African American students, some readers may be surprised to learn that while excellent schools are rare, they are not difficult to find. They thrive in plain sight. They challenge the Achievement Gap every day. All that is required is for us to look for them, identify them, study their methods for success, and apply those strategies.

As noted in the introduction to the Second Edition, I have identified and examined 11 predominantly African American public schools in California, each characterized by high rates of poverty. To find our schools, I looked at enrollment demographics and data. I tracked how many students were African American, and how many qualified for free and reduced-price meals. From there, I reviewed the 2015-2017 California Assessment of Student Performance and Progress, known as CAASPP.

To qualify for the study, each school was required to have an enrollment that included at least 49 percent African American students – more than eight times the statewide average of six percent African American. I focused on schools where more than half of the students qualified for free or reduced meals. Finally, I looked for schools that scored above the statewide CAASPP average in English Language Arts for African American students, which is 31 percent. Almost half of the 11 schools performed at or above the statewide ELA average for all students, regardless of ethnicity.

The parameters ensured that our schools were high performing campuses with defined percentages of students who met or exceeded proficiency in English Language Arts or mathematics on the California standardized tests. Statistically, our qualifications were fulfilled, from ethnicity to income to academic excellence. Nine of the schools examined in the Second Edition operate as charters.

Predictably, the research revealed several commonalities and generalizations. Consistent themes quickly emerge at schools that bridge the Achievement Gap, especially as those themes relate to site leadership, teacher interventions and parental or guardian involvement.

As for general observations, I offer them in random order of significance:

1. The 11 schools tended to have smaller enrollments than most inner-city schools attended by the students' peers.

2. Each school had a site leader with a vision and plan based upon the expectation that every student will succeed.

3. Teachers were selected based on their belief that this unique cohort can succeed, with a willingness to show progress toward that goal.

4. Parents made the choice and commitment to assist students at home and support the school.

5. Instructional strategies were based upon frequent student assessments and adjustments to instructional strategies as indicated.

6. Professional development was available for teachers, including time reserved for peer collaboration.

7. Technology was deployed for classroom instruction and at home, and for family communications, data analysis and public information.

8. Students who needed extra time for instruction received it.

9. College and career ambitions were encouraged with meaningful experiences.

10. Parents received learning opportunities, in person and on-line, to enrich their involvement in their children's education.

11. Community supporters were engaged, notably people with track records for delivering services and resources to families, students, and schools.

In addition to the research conducted at each school site, I reviewed works by other researchers who have explored the Achievement Gap for African American students. Here's what some of those researchers have to say:

1. *Rising African American Student Achievement: California Goals, Local Outcomes*, EdSource, a California non-profit (2008).

This report provides a state-level overview of the academic achievement in English Language Arts and mathematics for California's African American students in elementary grades through the high school years, plus a brief look at community college attainment. The report confirms the existence of the Achievement Gap at every level. It uses as key indicators the Academic Performance Index, the percentage completion of "A to G" college preparatory courses, and high school graduation rates. The study provides noteworthy observations about the distribution of African American students in California. It found that in 2007, two-thirds of California's 477,800 African American students lived in just five of the state's 58 counties – Los Angeles (35 percent), San Bernardino (10 percent), Sacramento (eight percent), Alameda (seven percent), and San Diego (seven percent). Further, two-thirds of all African American students in the most populated county – Los Angeles – attend school in just four of that county's 80 elementary, unified and high school districts (Los Angeles Unified, Long Beach Unified, Compton Unified and Inglewood Unified).

The 23-page report has an excellent description of the distribution of African American students across a few counties, districts and schools in California. Notably, the report contains examples of high academic achievement growth among African American students at every level, though the overall Achievement Gap trend remains in effect. The report finds that 45 elementary schools had an African American Growth API of 785 or higher in 2007. Similarly, 18 middle schools had an African American Growth API of at least 748. Finally, 16 high schools had an African American Growth API of 736 or more. These 45 elementary, 18 middle and 16 high schools scored well above the average: at least 1.5 standard deviations above the mean for their respective school levels.

The point is that this large-scale study – like our own examination – documents the existence of schools where African American students perform at acceptable, if not exceptional, levels despite the general statewide trend toward relatively poor performance. The study provides the perspective that a statewide strategy to close the Achievement Gap could encompass five counties and a small number of school districts and reach a large portion of California's African American students. This comprehensive study is worthy of review.

The full EdSource report contains interviews with more than a dozen school principals with high achievement among African American students. It can be seen at the website EdSource.org.

2. *African American Student Performance in Charter Schools Overview,* California Charter Schools Association (2017).

This is part of a series of examinations that includes "Portrait of the Movement Reports," published by the CCSA, which chronicles the performance of students enrolled in charter schools over a five-year period.

The 2017 report tracks the annual enrollments of African American students in California charter schools from 2008, when there were 30,119 students, thru 2017, when the number increased to 48,154 African American students. The report concludes that in 2016-17, more African American students attended charter public schools than traditional district schools in eight large urban California school districts.

Beyond enrollment trends, there are important findings regarding academic achievement. The report found a greater percentage of African American students in charter schools met or exceeded standards on the state's Smarter Balanced Assessment Consortium exam than their peers in traditional public schools. The study also found that in every school district examined, African American charter public schools students are more likely to complete "A to G" courses than their peers at traditional schools. "A to G" courses are a set of 15, one-year college prep courses high school students must take to be eligible for either the California State University or University of California systems. Moreover, graduation rates that tracked all students in the ninth through 12th grades showed that in a majority of districts, charter students are more likely to graduate high school in four years.

In the 2016-17 school year:

Ninety-five percent of African American students attending Sacramento City Unified charter high schools graduated, as opposed to only 68 percent at district's traditional schools.

Sixty-three percent of African American students attending Los Angeles Unified charter high schools graduated, as opposed to 50 percent at traditional public schools.

Sixty-two percent of African American students attending Oakland Unified charter high schools graduated, as opposed to 57 percent at traditional public schools.

Stanford University's Center for Research on Education Outcomes, the nation's foremost independent analyst of charter school effectiveness, has release several comprehensive reports that offer unprecedented insight into the effectiveness of charter schools, especially as they relate to African American students.

The center's "Urban Charter Study of 2015" documented that African American students in charter schools in California's urban centers gain weeks and months of additional learning as a result of being in charter schools. Among the findings:

- In the Bay Area, African American charter school students gain more than three months in reading and more than four months in math.

- In Central California, African American charter school students gain more than two months in reading and more than seven weeks in math.

- In the South Bay, African American charter school students gain more than four weeks in reading and more than ten weeks in math.

- In Southern California, African American charter school students gain more than 26 days in reading and more than 36 days in math.

The center conducted an analysis of public data on suspensions in California in 2014 and 2015. On average, California charter schools suspend students at the same or lower rates than traditional public schools. The research show similar rates for elementary schools, but significantly lower suspension rates for middle schools and high schools. For African American students, the out-of-school suspension rates in charter schools are only about half of traditional school suspension rates.

There was significant controversy in 2017 over a suggestion that a moratorium be placed on the growth of charter schools at the national level and in California. Oddly, some proponents of this nonsense are otherwise reputable organizations. But if the purpose is to better serve traditionally low achieving students – especially African American students – the proponents of a moratorium should be asked to respond publicly to the findings of these studies. Rather, I suspect that there are other motives at work here – motives that have nothing to do with the Achievement Gap or considering what is best for African American children. In any case, while the authors of these studies hasten to point out that more work needs to be done to bring scale to the promising practices, the last thing policy makers should do is inhibit the growth of worthwhile and effective educational practices for African American students. I trust that research studies such as the ones cited in the Second Edition receive consideration in the court of public opinion.

3. *National Charter Management Organization Study,* Center for Research on Education Outcomes (2017).

This study uses data from 2011-2012 to 2014-2015 school years across twenty-four states, plus New York City and Washington, D.C.

The findings show that attendance at a charter school that is part of a larger network of schools indicates improved educational outcomes for students.

Key findings:

- Charter school organizations have their strongest effects with traditionally underserved populations, such as Black and Hispanic students.

Number of schools	63,616 traditional	and 5,786 charter
Percent Black	13% traditional	and 27% charter
Percent White	48% traditional	and34% charter

- Black students attending charter schools have significantly stronger outcomes than African American students attending traditional public schools, in both reading and math, especially if they attend a Charter Management Organization school. These students gain the equivalent of an additional 34 days in math and 29 additional days of learning.

- Charter school operators with non-profit status have significantly higher student academic gains than for-profit operators.

4. *Sweating The Small Stuff: Inner City Schools and the New Paternalism*, David Whitman, Thomas B. Fordham Institute (2008).

This book reviews six inner-city secondary schools that are bridging or have bridged the Achievement Gap. Four are public charter schools; one is a traditional district school; one is a Catholic school.

Many traits of these schools are not surprising. They are academically rigorous. They have high expectations. They provide extra core instructional time, either by extending the school day or year (or both), or by reducing electives, assemblies, announcements and other diversions during the school day.

5. *Teaching As Leadership: The Highly Effective Teacher's Guide To Closing The Achievement Gap,* Stephan Farr. Jossey Bass (2010).

This book tells the experiences of several Teach for America graduates and defines what these teachers, who are new to their profession, are doing to bridge the Achievement Gap. Teachers quoted in the work believe that bringing equal opportunities to all children in the United States is not an insurmountable goal. The 2005 National Teacher of the Year, Jason Kamras, said, "It all comes down to people. Effective teachers – those who not only have the highest expectations for their students, but who also know how to help them reach those expectations – are the most important piece of the puzzle."

6. *Promising Practices for Teaching Algebra I: Portraits of Successful Teachers of African American and Latino Students,* M. Davis, S. Lee and R. Dorph. The Lawrence Hall of Science, University of California Berkeley (unpublished, 2010).

This research reports on seven case studies of successful teachers from six California high schools and one middle school. The schools had between 25 to 100 percent Hispanic students, or 20 to 50 percent African American students. They were selected because their California Standards Test scores in Algebra I were high compared to other schools, and combined enrollment of African American and Hispanic students was at least 50 percent.

The authors explain how successful teachers establish clear practices and procedures in their classrooms. The teachers were explicit about their high expectations for assigned activities and remained consistent in their expectations. Constant monitoring of student progress was instrumental. All teachers in the study emphasize problem-solving skills and push students to develop both procedural fluency and a conceptual understanding of the methods they use to solve problems. Teachers took responsibility for whether or not their students learned. With respect to school leadership, principals built schedules to allow more time – extra minutes of instruction for students who needed it. Another key part of school leadership is the effort to increase teacher collaboration.

7. *Closing the Achievement Gap for African American Students: Best Practices for Student Success,* Total School Solutions, Association of California School Administrators, and California Association of African American Superintendents and Administrators, Pre-Conference (2010).

This reference is a collection of presentations at the Total School Solutions, ACSA and CAAASA conference. Many schools described their evidence of success and cited various program strategies to obtain success. One example was Think College Now, an elementary school in Oakland. This kindergarten to fifth grade school had 95 percent free or reduced meals and 81 percent Hispanic and African American enrollment.

The description of the Think College Now theory of action included these highlights:

- The entire community was united in the early college focus mission.

- High expectations for all students, staff, parents – no excuses.

- Standards-based, data-driven instruction and assessment.

- Strong family involvement and community partnerships.

- Outstanding staff with a sense of urgency to reach goals.

Think College Now was selected as a California Distinguished School and won the Title I Academic Achievement Award.

8. *Whatever It Takes,* Paul Tough. First Mariner Books (2008).

Paul Tough describes the experiences of Geoffrey Canada, founder of the Harlem Children's Zone, and his creation of a series of inter-connected social services organizations and schools to serve impoverished children in New York City.

At Promise Academy middle school, reading scores in 2009 showed that 58 percent of eighth-grade students were at or above grade level, which was higher than the New York City average. For math, 87 percent of students in eighth grade scored at or above grade level, higher than both state and city averages.

President Barack Obama declared the centerpiece of his urban-poverty work would be to replicate the Harlem Children Zone in 20 cities across America. He would call these "Promise Neighborhoods."

9. *Results of Four State Study: Smaller Schools Reduce Harmful Impact of Poverty on Student Achievement,* C. Howley and R. Bickel, The Rural School and Community Trust (2009). Website: ruraledu.org

This study focuses on the interaction between poverty and enrollment size. It concludes that poorer schools benefit from smaller enrollments.

10. *Small Schools: A Reform That Works,* Mary Anne Raywid. Educational Leadership (1997).

Large-scale studies compared the records of 300 students in eight small New York schools prior to and after entrance. The studies examined the records of 20,000 students in Philadelphia's public high schools, comparing small and large school student performance, and examined the test scores of 13,000 students in Alaska.

Other studies involved nearly 12,000 students in 800 high schools nationwide. These studies consistently found that small-school students did better academically than students in larger schools. This was particularly the case for disadvantaged students. Size had more influence on student achievement than any other factor controllable by educators. The impact of size held steady at all grade levels, from elementary through high school. Besides positive effects on student achievement, small schools have other benefits. At-risk students are more likely to achieve in small schools. There is less violence. Students display more social concern in small schools, and dropout rates are reduced.

———

My research for this Second Edition of *Bridging the Achievement Gap* corroborated by studies listed above, calls to mind the *Effective Schools Research*, published in 1979 by the late Dr. Ronald Edmonds, former Director of the Center for Urban Studies at Harvard's graduate education program, 1973-77. Dr. Edmonds' six characteristics are very similar to my own list cited above.

Ultimately, this discussion about research reminds me of Ron Edmonds' thesis, which has been quoted by many educators over the years.

Dr. Edmonds said, "We can, whenever and wherever we choose, successfully teach all children whose schooling is of interest to us. Whether or not we do this depends upon how we feel about the fact that we haven't done it so far."

I'll return to this point in the Conclusion.

The Second Edition research also corroborated conclusions by the Stanford University Center for Research on Education Outcomes (CREDO), which found that "attending a charter school that is part of a larger network of schools is associated with improved educational outcomes for students." CREDO found that charter school organizations have their strongest impact with traditionally under-served populations, such as African American and Latino students.

As the tables in the Appendix demonstrate, high-performing charter schools can significantly benefit African American students. Six of the nine charters described in this book are run by Charter Management Organizations. The impressive assessments produced by schools operated under the KIPP Los Angeles, St. HOPE and Fortune management groups support the CREDO findings.

Several other observations about the schools identified in this research are noteworthy. First, the highest performing school is Wilder's Prep Academy, which is a charter school not operated under a CMO. The second-highest performing school, Cowan Elementary, is a traditional school, not a charter. Two schools in our study are "traditional" public schools, not charters. Those schools, Baldwin Hills Elementary and Cowan Avenue, were designated as "magnet" sites, which allow them to offer unique and diverse curriculum while they draw students from beyond neighborhood boundaries. These schools reflect several features found at charters, but they are in most respects operated as traditional public schools in the Los Angeles Unified School District.

The larger lesson is how a handful of California public schools have managed to produce consistently strong academic performances among African American students. They bridge the Achievement Gap while most other public schools fail. Chapter One provides narrative descriptions about how these successful sites work – and what steps other schools can take to replicate the positive results.

What are the implications of the Charter Management Organization comparisons?

As described at the end of Chapter One, the business of operating a charter school is complex. It calls for thoughtful leadership about how to strike a balance between site-level flexibility and direction from headquarters. There are justifications for tightly run

Charter Management Organizations. And there are pros and cons about letting each campus design and operate its own model.

In 2011, author Jay Mathews, in his bestseller, "Work Hard, Be Nice: How Two Inspired Teachers Created the Most Promising Schools in America," described the KIPP organization as having 66 schools in 19 states and the District of Columbia, including schools in nine of the 10 largest U.S. cities. The author noted that 1,400 students at 28 KIPP schools in 22 cities improved, on average, from the 34th to 58th percentile in reading between the fifth and seventh grades. In math, they improved on average from the 33rd to 83rd percentile. Such gains were unprecedented, Mathews wrote. About 80 percent of KIPP students are from low-income families. Around 95 percent are African American and Latino.

The St. HOPE Public Schools (three schools, K-12) and Fortune School of Education (seven schools, transitional kindergarten-12) have far fewer schools and have been operating for fewer years than the KIPP program. The operational model for St. HOPE resembles KIPP. The tightly managed Fortune model is found in communities similar to KIPP. The Fortune organization believes consistency across a small model helps parents who must move from one part of town to another. The schools they find in their old and new neighborhoods are very much the same.

It must be noted that the independent charter schools included on our list of high-performing schools – even schools without a CMO – enjoyed the benefits of longevity. Watts Learning Center has operated for two decades as a charter school. Wilder's Prep Academy was approved as a charter more than 15 years ago. Moreover, Wilder ran as a private school for 23 years before it became a charter.

Clearly, the experienced leadership at Watts Learning Center and Wilder had years to fine-tune their general business functions, even without a Charter Management Organization. The absence of such experience has caused many startup charters to fail.

How can the successful practices from several charter and traditional schools benefit hundreds of California schools?

Replicating the best practices of excellent schools can only happen with the determination to change the narrative that underscores the failure of African American students. What would it take to insist that low-performing schools – sites that have not achieved the levels of proficiency found at the 11 schools featured here – examine the strategies perfected at successful schools? What would it take for neighborhood schools and their communities to adopt proven strategies to overcome the Achievement Gap?

Such questions should be raised with districts and schools that would receive the supplemental funding called for in Assembly Bill 2635, described in the conclusion of this book.

With or without the adoption of new legislation, the Achievement Gap can be bridged only with collaboration and commitment among informed and determined stakeholders. The 11 schools examined here – undaunted by historical challenges and inspired by their students, parents, teachers, and administrators – provide living proof.

Three

The Innovators:

Prescribe the culture.

Hold people accountable

Bridging the Achievement Gap requires cooperation, collaboration and hard work from countless diverse and dedicated people, both professional and lay. But the work starts at the top, with organizational leadership. In this chapter, three chief executives from California Charter Management Organizations discuss their missions and strategies.

'Our goal is to prepare students for college'
An interview with Marcia Aaron, CEO of KIPP Los Angeles Public Schools:

Some researchers point to greater success by charter schools operating under a non-profit Charter Management Organization (CMO) than those operating independently, without a CMO. Why do CMO schools tend to be more successful?

Many administrative and support functions are taken off the plates of principals in the KIPP Los Angeles regional charter schools. For example, this includes recruiting and screening of personnel, data analysis, community outreach, financial development and alumni support. As a result, KIPP LA charter principals can focus on instructional leadership and support for teachers. In an independent charter, the principal-founder would have to attend to all of those functions, and could not focus as much on the quality of instruction.

Of the various services you provide for each of your charter schools, which do you think make the greatest difference?

Leadership development is a key priority. The success of our teachers to offer an instructional program that will prepare our students for college and careers depends upon having strong principals on the campuses.

What services provided by your CMO would an independent charter school have difficulty managing?

The KIPP LA regional office provides coaching for principals. We have staff assigned to manage a cluster of schools to help them meet external requirements, such as preparation of the Local Control Achievement Plan. My staff assists schools with facilities acquisition and maintenance. Regional staff is invested in data management and the use of data to improve programs. At the regional level, we do follow-up studies on students as they matriculate through high school and college. Again, an independent charter school is not likely to have the capacity to perform all of these functions.

Consider an independent group that might have options to establish more than one charter school. What are the most critical details they must attend to?

First, employ instructional leaders. Even though our schools are K-8, our goal is to prepare students for college. To realize this goal, each school needs a strong instructional leader as principal. Second, employ someone who has fiscal management acumen. Beyond awareness of the overall budget, cash flow management requires more fiscal sophistication to be able live within available resources.

As you consider the future, what are the most pressing goals for your CMO?

The Los Angeles KIPP regional office oversees and provides services to 17 schools. Given our emphasis upon quality school leadership, we want to develop a pipeline of future leaders, taking into account quality teachers or other leaders already within our system. We will strengthen and develop new relations with community partners – including universities – to help us achieve that goal.

For more information on KIPP LA, visit the website http://www.kippla.org.

'We set the tone for learning'

An interview with Dr. Margaret Fortune, President and CEO of Fortune School of Education:

Some research points to greater success by charter schools operating under a non-profit Charter Management Organization than those operating independently without a CMO. Why do you think this is so?

My familiarity with this research has to do with new charter schools. New charters tend to be more successful if they are opened by a CMO than if they are a single charter school. I think that's true because the Charter Management Organizations have more capacity: back office, curriculum and instruction. Many of them, like Fortune

School of Education, are replicating a model. We are well resourced enough to choose our leaders for a year ahead of time and to have them employed and working on the school that they know they are going to open. And they are not doing that in isolation. They are doing that with the support of budget, facilities, human resources, curriculum and instruction – all of the component parts of opening a school.

What are some of the challenges that face an independent charter?

Sometimes, when you have a single operator, that person might be an excellent educator, but not well versed on the business of running schools. That can be overwhelming. Typically, charter schools that struggle financially do so because school finance is a complicated affair. And there are lots of ways to go wrong and get yourself into some trouble. I think that's one thing that CMOs have greater capacity than a single school operator. Some people will say that for a charter management organization, your next school is an opportunity to perfect your model even further. When you are on school Number One, it's very different than being on school Number Seven. It's not your first rodeo when you are on school Number Seven. You have the advantage of learning from your mistakes and perfecting the model so that the next time you implement it, it's even better than the first or the second or third or whatever it is for you. Those are some reasons why a CMO would be higher performing than an independent school, especially at the beginning.

Of the various strategies that you bring to each of your schools, which do you think makes the greatest difference?

The consistency of our back office functions takes a huge load off of our schools, everything from school finance to attendance to data and analytics to human resources to food service. There are lots of different aspects to running a school and we have lots of support around those functions. In addition, I think that our commitment to professional development, which really is extraordinary, helps our schools. We have weekly principal's meetings, and those are weekly opportunities for professional development. We also have weekly professional development for teachers with their grade level across schools in the network led by master teachers. We have lots of observation instruments where our goal is to get better faster. We are very analytical in our approach and pay a lot of attention to detail and that is across the board, but in particular on our curriculum.

What role does managerial consistency play?

It makes a big difference to have consistency across the buildings. Our model is to implement adopted instructional materials with fidelity. We also have a very clear culture that's based on what we call the Five Pillars: high expectations, choice and commitment, more time, focus on results, and citizenship. Having a clear education philosophy and a clear vision helps the whole organization to maintain mission alignment. We attract people who are passionate about closing the African American Achievement Gap, because that's our "why." That's why we've opened these schools, so we tend to attract people who care deeply about that. I think all of these things make a difference for the schools that are a part of our network.

Are there services provided by your CMO that independent charters would likely not be able to step up to?

Our CMO is unique in that we have a graduate school of education where we credential our own teachers and principals. Having this ability to license teachers, within that strong muscle around professional development, goes as a leg up in the recruitment and preparation of teachers. It also gives educators a career ladder and it gives us a way to prepare leaders, which allows us to grow. If you want to grow schools in order to green-light projects, there are certain things that you need. One of the most important things that you need is the leader. The fact that we have the ability to credential our own principals is really significant in the growth of our organization. We are able to this because we serve a consortium of school districts, over 60 districts, not just ourselves. If we were a single charter school we would likely not have the capacity to have that type of operation going concurrently with our charter school network.

Does scale allow you to avoid contracting out for services?

Another advantage we have involves our ability to do things in-house. Many small charter schools that are single campuses may contract out some functions that we have in-house. They might go to a company for back office support, whereas that's something that we have internally. In fact, before we ever opened a single charter school, we had our whole CMO staff in place, so we had far more capacity than we needed to operate a single school. While that capacity has grown over time, the capacity that we had on Day One probably took us through opening three schools. Now that we have seven schools, we've certainly expanded our back office. But when you do those functions internally, it allows you to control the quality and make sure that the mission alignment is in every aspect of your organization.

Can you give an example?

For a time, we contracted out our custodial services. And the execution of custodial services was very poor. One part of our philosophy is high expectations, and that applies to everything. We expect to have the cleanest schools in America. And you can't have high expectation if you are contracting out a function like that. You are really only as good as the contractor that you hired, and in our case, that contractor wasn't very good. And when we brought that function in-house, that allowed us to do a few things. It allowed us to pay custodians more. We went from $10 an hour to $15 an hour: a living wage. It allowed us to give full-time custodians full-time benefits for themselves and their family with no employee contribution, which is the same way we treat our teachers. It allowed us to put those custodians in uniforms that reflected our brand. It allowed us to provide them professional development like we do other key members of our team. As the CMO, we have enough need to have a whole custodial staff and custodial supervisor and director of maintenance. Bringing that function in-house made it stronger than it was when we were just operating one or two schools and really couldn't afford to have those functions run to the level that we do now as a CMO. The other things I'll say on that point, one of the developers in town that I took note of had a philosophy of vertical alignment, and that is that his mission was to control every aspect of the development project and not contract anything out. Again, it's another example of wanting to control quality. That developer was the late Buzz Oates, a big name in Sacramento.

Considering an independent school that might have an option to establish more than one charter school, what are the most critical details that must be attended to?

First, the group has to be really clear about what their model is. They need to be able to articulate it in terms of their education philosophy. For example, as noted earlier, Fortune School is guided by the Five Pillars: high expectations, choice and commitment, more time, focus on results, and citizenship. Everything that we do is aligned to that philosophy. We have three simple rules: listen, respect, and work hard. Those are philosophical beliefs.

The instructional model is something you also have to be clear about. How does your school do school? There are some schools that are International Baccalaureate programs. There are some schools that are Montessori programs. Fortune is a program with an instructional model that relies on a highly rigorous curriculum that is designed for kids to be college and career ready. We execute that with fidelity. We set the tone for learning by a very disciplined culture of high expectations, which essentially amounts to very clear routines and procedures for adults and children in schools.

How urgent is the establishment of an instructional model?

Before you open a single school, you have to be clear about what your instructional model is. And certainly, that's true if you intend to do multiple schools. The other thing that an organization that wants to open schools has to attend to is whether it is running a tight model or a loose model, and there are CMO's that are all along the spectrum. Some CMO's are tight, like Fortune School of Education. We're replicating a model. We prescribe what the curriculum is. We prescribe what the culture is. We hold people accountable for that. All of the school's employees work for Fortune School. The principals are a part of a team; they are not independent agents. They are executing out a model. That's a tight model. Then there are looser models where you might say, "We want your test scores to look like this, and we're going to establish a goal around that and we're not going to prescribe how you get there. You choose your curriculum. You choose your culture. You choose your theme. As long as you meet these test scores, we're fine." And that will be an example of a loose model.

The group that may want to open schools needs to decide how they are going to function along that spectrum. There are philosophical things that have to do with planning. There are other things that are practical considerations, like who's your authorizer going to be? All charter schools have to be approved by an authorizing school district, county office, or State Department of Education. What is that political environment? Do you have the political chops to get a charter petition passed?

Are politics more important than merit for a charter school application?

A successful charter application is mostly based on merit. The part of it that is political, even if you have an application with merit, can undermine the whole enterprise when you are not in command of the politics. You have to think through that. Then, there is the practical consideration of the facility. If you are going to run a school, you need to control your building. Then, special education is also something that is a consideration for those looking to get into charter schools. I think you want to control special education rather than contracting out, even to a district that authorizes you. There are lots of decisions to be made and it's not something to be gone into lightly, for sure. It's an expensive enterprise but it's also doable if the group is interested and dedicated, not just for now, but for the long term.

As you consider the future, what are the most pressing goals for your Charter Management Organization?

Fortune has authority to operate 10 charter schools, one in San Bernardino and another nine in Sacramento. We currently have seven campuses, and we have three more to go. We will have met our charge to have an entire school network with 10 schools. The next schools that are on the horizon will be based on demand for new schools. We have K-5 schools, K-8 schools, a middle school, as well as a high school. A new middle school will likely open in the 2019-2020 school year. Beyond charter schools, on the horizon is a new development in higher education, which is regional accreditation for our teacher-education programs. That accreditation will help us to open a Historically Black College on the West Coast. Finally, we're working on a system of private pre-schools that are based on the Regul model, which is a philosophy around early education based on play and literacy. When these new systems are implemented, the

Fortune School of Education will have the whole preschool through college continuum.

Fortune School of Education is a network of tuition-free, public charter schools in California, created to close the Achievement Gap by preparing students for college starting in kindergarten. At the early college high school, students can earn their high school diploma and their associate degrees at the same time. We partner with Consumes River College in South Sacramento, and California State Polytechnic University in San Luis Obispo. We have partnerships with the African American press. In Sacramento, our partner is the Sacramento Observer newspaper, and in San Bernardino our partner is the Black Voice. The Fortune School of Education also provides credentialing programs for teachers and administrators. Our schools are headquartered in Sacramento. We have campuses in Sacramento and San Bernardino counties, which include the second and third largest African American student populations in California, respectively.

The Fortune School Organization:

There were seven schools in 2018, including a K-8 and a new high school that opened in August 2017. The schools in order of their founding:
Fortune School (K-5th grades)
6829 Stockton Boulevard, Suite 380, Sacramento, CA 95823
William Lee College Prep (K-5th grades)
3300 Stockton Boulevard, Sacramento, CA 95820
Alan Rowe College Prep (K-6th grades)
9424 Big Horn Boulevard, Elk Grove, CA 95758
Ephraim Williams College Prep Middle School (6th-8th grades)
4545 9th Avenue, Sacramento, CA 95820
Hazel Mahone College Prep (K-5th grades)
3750 Rosin Court, Sacramento, CA 95834
Rex and Margaret Fortune Early College High School (9th-12th grades)
9270 Bruceville Road, Elk Grove, CA 95758

Hardy Brown College Prep (K-8th grades)
655 West 2nd Street, San Bernardino, CA 92415

For more information, visit the website https://www.fortuneschool.us

'We allow them to determine how they get there'

An interview with Jake Mossawir, CEO of St. HOPE Public Schools, which runs three schools in the Oak Park community of Sacramento:

Research has suggested that charter schools operating under a non-profit Charter Management Organization have greater success than those operating independently. Why do you think this is so?

In my experience, operating a small Charter Management Organization provides three key opportunities that allow for greater success: economies of scale, research and development and compliance streamlining.

Can you take them one at a time?

I'll start with economies of scale. The regulatory burden and operational needs of a single independent charter school are virtually the same as that of a CMO. As such, the ability to share those costs and resources becomes a huge advantage. Whether purchasing supplies in bulk at better rates or submitting state reports via a shared staff member, economies of scale allow our school leaders to do more with their budgets. As for research and development, charter schools were founded with the idea of innovation. Having a handful of schools for us to test different strategies and approaches allows our school leaders to learn from one another and ultimately makes our network stronger. Finally, there's compliance streamlining. Between federal, state and local regulations, the burden of compliance would be crippling to a school leader who wants to focus on academics. The ability of a CMO to pull those aspects of the work off of a school leader's plate allows them to spend more time in the classroom, focusing on professional development and other important matters.

Of the various services you provide for each of your charter schools, which do you think make the greatest difference?

It will sound somewhat contradictory, but we provide autonomy. One might ask, "How does a CMO provide autonomy?" Well, the answer is, by creating freedom within a framework. We want our school leaders to ultimately be the "CEOs" of their schools. As a CMO, our job is to make sure they are able to operate in a legally compliant way, within their budgets and ensuring that ultimately students are successful. Our job is to provide our school leaders with the resources they need to ensure student achievement. But we allow them to determine how they get there.

Are there services provided by your Charter Management Organization that independent charter schools would not likely to be able to manage on their own?

My experience is somewhat limited in this category, but what I will say is that an independent charter can probably provide many of the services we provide. But I believe the scale of a CMO allows us to do more with those services by pooling resources and leveraging one another.

If an independent group has options to establish more than one charter school, what are the most critical details they must attend to?

The biggest areas would be determining their management structure, which services are centralized, how school leaders will be held accountable and how to ensure teacher and staff input into decisions. Ultimately, understanding which decisions and responsibilities sit at the school level vs. the CMO is probably the biggest day-to-day operational consideration.

As you consider the future, what are the most pressing goals for your CMO?

Our goals are always going to lead, first and foremost, with student achievement. We want to ensure that our students are prepared to excel as they enter the next grade. Additionally, we have been working over the last four years with a few different partner organizations to support our students in completing college. There is also room for us to continue to refine our network-wide academic alignment and professional learning. Finally, we also strive for operational excellence. The stronger our operations are, the more time and resources can be provided to our students.

For more information about the St. HOPE organization, visit the website http://www.sthope.org/public-schools-home.

Four

The Parents:

'We listened to our parents in our community'

I am a professional educator with more than 50 years of experience as a teacher, site leader and school district administrator. I admire people who devote their careers to teaching. But over the decades, I have come to realize that one critical component in the successful education of young people originates from somewhere else — a place beyond the training, credentials and experience that define our best professional teachers.

While skilled, motivated and collaborative classroom management is essential for every student's academic success, there is another part of the equation that is often overlooked or minimized: the role of the parent or guardian.

In my experience, the parent's contribution is frequently dismissed due to the fact that it can't be easily quantified, mandated or predicted. We can't count on it, so we rarely factor it into our professional protocols. Parents become deeply involved or disengaged from their students' education for countless reasons. But when they choose to participate in the school experience, it's typically for three reasons: They love their children. They want them to thrive academically. They are encouraged to participate thanks to a genuinely welcoming and supportive environment at school.

This chapter is devoted to parents who have elected to become participants in their children's education. They have blocked out the time, made the sacrifices, educated themselves in the curriculum and partnered with teachers, site leaders and their young people to provide the support, guidance and faith that helps create a seamless environment from school to home — a relentless loop of learning.

To more deeply explore the significance of parental involvement, I met with parents and guardians, teachers and administrators from three schools examined in my study. Each school has significant numbers of families with low incomes, a high percentage of African American students enrolled and impressive scores on state-administered standardized tests. The schools I focused on for this chapter are Oak Park Prep Academy in Sacramento, Watts Learning Center in Los Angeles and Fortune School in Sacramento.

Oak Park Prep Academy

Let's begin with Annie Cervenka, the principal who introduced us to her middle school staff and students at Oak Park Prep. Cervenka described a weekly method of communication with parents. It involves the "Green Folder." With no trappings of technology, the Green Folder is exactly what the name suggests: a folder sent home to parents with the expectation that they will read, sign and return it to school after discussing the contents with their students. The Green Folder contains information about grades, behavior and any newsletter information the principal or teacher wishes parents to know. A second method for communication between parents and teachers at Oak Park Prep does involve tech. It's an online commercial program called "ClassDojo." The Dojo platform allows teachers to inform parents — by the hour if necessary — of extraordinary events involving their students, not just misbehavior, but special achievements or awards. Several teachers at Oak Park Prep use Dojo to communicate daily with parents.

Approximately 65 percent of Oak Park Prep parents use Dojo. The platform is easy to master, which helps boost participation. When asked how frequently parents attend school meetings or events, Cervenka noted the average falls to between 25 and 40 percent. The attendance numbers climb for special events, such as "back to school" nights and student-led parent conferences. Encouraging for Oak Park staff are the large numbers of parents who attend special "oral history" nights. In tracking student performance and dealing with issues such as misbehavior, the principal and teachers described the overall level of parent involvement as "high."

Consistent engagement by parents at Oak Park Prep is a priority for the administration and staff, but it becomes more difficult as children grow older. The school serves students in the sixth, seventh and eighth grades — years that typically see parent involvement decline as students become more independent. At my visits, I did not notice any parents coming and going, unlike at my tours of elementary schools.

Overall, Oak Park Prep educators are proud of their parental communication and involvement and consider the strong connection between home and classroom as a substantial contributor to the school's success.

Watts Learning Center

Jabahara Henry is the father of a third-grade student at Watts Learning Center, which serves children in kindergarten through fifth grade. Henry obtained a math text and supporting materials, including audiotapes, from his child's teacher. At home after school, he reviews each day's lesson with his daughter. Very quickly, he noticed the review process resulted in stronger classroom performances by his daughter. He attributes her success to the family's attention to routine and the father-daughter work regimen after school, with the focus on the same materials used by the teacher during class.

As the father of a young daughter, Henry exemplified some of the positive parenting practices I have described in a book that will be referenced later, *Parenting Practices: What Successful Parents Do*. The book's contents were based on my research in high performing, high minority schools. Watts Learning Center was among them.

Let me describe another parent from Watts Learning Center. Like Jabahara Henry, this parent has met with her child's teacher and collected instructional materials. She reviews every lesson with her daughter and spends about two hours each weekday helping her complete homework assignments. The parent volunteers at school. She believes her daughter benefits from the staff's familiarity with the family. The benefits clearly extend beyond the student. Mom reported she began taking her daughter to a local library after school on the teacher's advice. Books are selected just for fun, but they help build vocabulary. Over my career, I have frequently referenced vocabulary building as a positive parenting practice. In this case, mother and daughter collectively look up unfamiliar words at the library and use them in sentences — another example of parent engagement nudged forward by communication with a teacher.

A third parent from Watts Learning Center made reference to the school's policy of suggesting that parents volunteer 25 hours of service per academic year. The word "service" carries a broad definition, and can include working with a parent's own child or service at school. This parent gives more than 25 hours when she adds up the time spent volunteering at school and helping her own child at home. She assists various teachers in multiple classrooms, but occasionally helps her child's teacher — moments that bring pride and happiness to the youngster.

Other parents reported using flash cards at home to help their children retain math lessons and cue cards for help with sight words. I spoke with the mother of a fifth-grade student at Watts Learning Center who began attending the school in kindergarten. Over years, the student learned to take notes in class. The parent reads the notes daily, and uses them to discuss progress with the student.

These anecdotes reflect the wisdom and words of Eugene Fisher, who founded Watts Learning Center. He said, "When we designed the school, we did not try to impose on parents a preconceived educational program as much as we did to go to them and say, 'We want to help you to help your child to do well.' So we listened to parents in our community because we valued their opinions. We know that, in order to cultivate them as partners, we have to show respect to them and they will continue through their tenure at the school."

Throughout its two decades of service to its community, Watts Learning Center has made parent involvement a centerpiece of its success.

Fortune School

The Sacramento campus of Fortune School offers kindergarten through fifth grade to a predominately African American student body. Like the other schools under discussion, Fortune is a top performer, particularly on state-administered standardized tests. The school suggests 40 hours of volunteer service for parents, though the suggestion carries no penalty for families that fall short or choose not to participate. The principal, Odissa Nyong, estimates about 50 percent of Fortune parents reach the 40-hour threshold. And some exceed it.

The principal has devised several creative ways to encourage parent engagement. Chief among them is a club called "Donuts for Dads," which meets monthly at the school. The gatherings typically include a school tour and classroom visits, where children (or grandchildren) are present. While donuts and friendship provide an attraction, the meetings often allow the principal to hear valuable feedback on the children's experiences at school and home. A club called "Muffins for Moms" provides similar connections for women.

One woman who has found multiple ways to communicate with Fortune School is Frances Funches. She is over 70, and is the great aunt of two children who attend Fortune campuses. Funches is a member of the school site council and has attended every Parent Academy — a learning session for parents and guardians — since the children under her care were enrolled. Some of the presentations were repeat sessions, but repetition made no difference to Funches. She said she learned something from every meeting she attended, including presentations on Common Core and how parents can help at home with math and English.

I visited Funches at her home and noticed a stack of books on the dining room table. It was summer, and school was not in session, but the educational process continued in the Funches' home with trips to the library. The journey to find books was not a school assignment or part of a summer project. It was done for fun. A bulletin board sat in the dining area. Attendance awards and notices of good grades were tacked to the board. Nearby were a computer and printer, deployed for schoolwork or printing out information the children looked up online.

Another Fortune School parent, Onae Drayton, awakens her children each morning with church music and prays with them as they drive to school. The family sings together in the car. In addition to giving her children academic support, Drayton provides spiritual inspiration. She believes spiritual guidance helps promote her expectations of diligence, good behavior, and responsiveness.

Tia Pope looks forward to receiving a folder sent home with her fourth-grade student. The folder, like the "Green Folder" at Oak Park Academy, contains homework and school information and includes a place for parents to sign, indicating they have reviewed the material. Pope decided to extend the communication links with her child's teacher and sought out YouTube videos that offered tutoring tips for parents. When her daughter excels in class, she is rewarded with a weekend trip to a Six Flags amusement park.

As these examples illustrate, the opportunities and resources for parent involvement are endless, limited only by imagination, encouragement and willingness. Many parents look beyond school to balance the social experiences of their children. They join Girl Scouts and dance classes. They become involved with Alpha Phi Alpha and Alpha Kappa Alpha tutorial programs. The key element is a nurturing attitude from the school staff toward the parent — when professional educators create an environment that encourages parental engagement, the parents will respond.

Perspectives On Parent Involvement

We now turn to a more generalized discussion of parent involvement. To set the framework, please consider my comments at a public hearing on the Local Control Accountability Plan regulations before the California State Board of Education in January 2014 at Sacramento:

> "President Kirst, Members of the Board, Superintendent Torlakson:
>
> *"I am Rex Fortune a retired educator and active member of the Sacramento community.*
>
> *"Thank you for recognizing the importance of parent involvement as part of the Local Control Accountability Plan (LCAP) template. This recommendation is to extend the language regarding parent involvement cited in the template to include parent training. The primary purpose of the proposed parent training should be to improve the*

*ability of parents to assist their children at home, taking
into account the Common Core standards as well as the
new Smarter Balanced testing.*

*"Districts and schools have appropriately established pro-
fessional development on theses topics for teachers and
other school staff. Likewise, parents need to have on-going
access to training that will prepare them to understand and
assist the instruction that their children are experiencing
in school.*

*"This inclusion of parent training in the LCAP, along with
an appropriate allocation of resources to support such
training, will increase the quality of parental involvement
in other areas called for in the template. Moreover, quality
training for parents will likely result in improved student
performance in school."*

I have referenced my research involving parents at high
minority, high performing schools, and described how they assist
their children's education. My book, *Parenting Practices: What
Successful Parents Do*, lists 12 practices.

Here's what successful parents do:

1. Develop their children's vocabulary from birth to kindergarten, including reading to them before they can talk.

2. Establish routines for more learning opportunities at home.

3. Teach their children at an early age that school is one place for
   learning. Home is another.

4. Engage fathers, or other males who are significant in the lives
   of the students, in the academic development of the children.

5. Establish and maintain multiple ways to communicate
   with teachers.

6. Monitor progress with schoolwork daily. Give praise where warranted. Arrange help when needed.

7. Demonstrate to children that learning is important, not just by what you say, but by what you do.

8. Establish good habits to support that learning at home takes precedence over TV, playing video games, listening to music, texting and use of social networks with friends on weeknights.

9. Provide a suitable place for children to learn at home.

10. Seek resources from the community or school to help children study effectively.

11. Consider tradeoffs that favor learning opportunities over expensive toys, clothes, games or other costly entertainment.

12. Consider yourself a learner and seek out opportunities to gain tips for parenting in magazines, books, school, on-line and community agencies.

Perspectives on Local Accountability

Parent involvement is an important part of education public policy. In California, school districts are required to produce a Local Control Accountability Plan, known as LCAP.

The LCAP addresses eight components, one of which is parent involvement. Much of the language describes the role parents play at schools, such as their participation in statutory committees or planning committees that lead toward the development of the LCAP. Beyond that, parent involvement varies across schools. Many successful schools have training programs or academies for parents.

Schools have long recognized the special interests of parents and the importance of their financial support. Booster groups supply funds and volunteer services for bands, sports, arts, music, dance and theater. Parents in booster clubs support their children and the school and become informed about their children's experiences. Beyond booster clubs, parent academies can help make parents and guardians aware of critical school practices and rules regarding attendance, behavior, curricular standards, graduation requirements and college admission.

Numerous organizations and websites publish materials to help parents understand their roles in school and at home. One such website is the "On-line Parent Academy" at www.FortuneandAssociates.com. The site contains more than 90 videos organized around the following topics:

1. Common Core: A principal describes the new emphasis of Common Core Standards.

2. Education Technology: A principal gives examples for parents to use at home.

3. Financial Aid: An administrator talks about applications for college funds.

4. Language Development: Teachers describe writing, reading, listening skills.

5. Math and Science: A teacher advises parents about careers in science.

6. Parent Involvement: Presenters cover the content of Chapter 4 in this book.

7. Student Attendance: Research on the impact of attendance on schooling.

8. Student Behavior and Discipline: Suggestions to parents for use at home.

9. Preparation for University and College: Admission officers advise parents.

10. Students With Special Needs: A director describes the program.

Personal Perspectives

Successful parent involvement starts at home and blossoms at school, with communication and encouragement from professional educators. While this chapter has been based on my experiences and research, it also reflects a personal side — my experience as a father and husband who, together with my wife Margaret, raised three children who became college graduates and went on to important work as adults.

But this starts our story mid-stream. My grandmother, Regina Fortune, was born before the first airplane took flight. She was a schoolteacher in North Carolina. Her parents were likely born in the late 1880s, not long after the adoption of the Reconstruction Amendments, the 13th, 14th and 15th Amendments to the U.S. Constitution, which ended slavery, granted citizenship and guaranteed African Americans the right to vote.

Historical Black Colleges began to open around that time. Regina graduated from one. Regina and Giles Fortune had six children, three of whom graduated from college and became public school teachers. One of Regina's children was my father, Rex C. Fortune, who became a teacher and principal of the high school from which I graduated.

My wife's parents were also educators. The four of them — her parents and mine — were born before World War I. They survived that war, the Great Depression and World War II. Three of them lived to vote for President John F. Kennedy, but none of them lived to vote for President Barack Obama. Frank Strait, my wife's father, died in 1950. But he and Margaret's mother, Dequilla Strait, instilled in my wife the value of education as a safeguard against poverty.

Margaret and I began our careers as teachers and administrators in the early 1960s. We raised our children to aim for careers requiring college educations, and we supported them to achieve that goal as our parents had done for us.

Our eldest daughter has two children, both of whom were in college prep programs in high school in 2018. From my story, you can account for five generations of parenting practices — spanning 125 years of the Fortune and Strait families — that have produced positive results for our family and many others.

One of our children, Margaret Fortune (II), has founded seven charter schools, which currently include some of our family's cultural teachings. Her schools serve nearly 2,000 students in Sacramento and San Bernardino Counties. Although Regina and Giles Fortune and the grandparents of my wife have long passed, their values for the pursuit of education — transmitted by their parenting practices through their children — live on in the experiences of their great-grand children. The takeaway is that parent involvement matters!

Vanessa Caigoy, Coordinator of Compliance for the Fortune School of Education, concluded a presentation on parent involvement with these words:

> "Ongoing research shows that parent involvement in schools improves student achievement, reduces absenteeism and restores parents' confidence in their children's education. Students with involved parents or other caregivers earn higher grades and test scores, have better social skills and show improved behavior."

Could not have said it better, Vanessa.

Five

The Solution:

A legislative answer to a generational problem

My goal for the Second Edition of *Bridging the Achievement Gap* was simple. I would identify a number of California public schools with high poverty and significant enrollments of African American students. Next, I would determine which of these schools were able to meet statewide proficiency levels in English Language Arts or mathematics at levels higher than their demographically aligned peers. Finally, I would examine each successful school and explore their backgrounds, cultures, strategies and practices.

I wanted to learn what people were doing right. I hoped to establish whether the best practices found at high performing, high poverty schools were consistent, quantifiable and suitable for replication at scale by similar schools across California and the United States.

The news media are often dominated by what doesn't work. I wanted to explore what does work.

Not surprisingly, I found affirmative answers to all of my questions. Yes, there are consistencies among top-performing schools. Yes, persistent best practices can be quantified. And yes, productive strategies can be duplicated at scale, provided schools and communities decide to follow time-proven pathways to success.

Based upon my decades of classroom and leadership experience and academic research, I have long believed the Achievement Gap can be bridged. People were doing the hard and necessary work as this sentence was being written. In this book, readers have met educators and community members who are making a difference. Unfortunately, the opposite is also true. Without the will to change, nothing will change.

My study began with California public schools whose enrollments include significant poverty and at least 50 percent African American students, or nearly eight times the statewide average. While I looked for schools with students who met proficiency in English or math at higher levels than their African American peers, I noted several such schools have managed to close the Achievement Gap on statewide averages for all students, without regard to ethnicity. The data suggest that these schools tend to be smaller than most inner-city schools.

As the presence of smaller sites suggests, there are specific themes associated with schools that close the Achievement Gap. Site leadership is a critical factor, as are teacher interventions and parent involvement. These three basic components – strong leadership, engaged teachers and parents who bring the educational experience home – would seem essential for progress against the Achievement Gap.

To be even more specific, I have laid out a series of best-practice themes consistent among top-performing schools. Without exception, these qualities were always present in schools that successfully bridged the Achievement Gap:

- School leaders with a vision and plan based upon the expectation that students can and will succeed.

- Teachers selected for their beliefs that students can and will succeed, and a willingness to show progress toward that goal.

- Parents who commit to assisting students at home and supporting the school.

- Instructional strategies based upon frequent assessments and adjustments to instructional strategies as necessary.

- Professional development for teachers and time allotted for peer collaboration.

- Tech platforms for instruction, family communications, data analysis and public information.

- Additional time for students who fall behind.

- Meaningful experiences to encourage aspiration for college and careers.

- Learning opportunities for parents, both in person and on-line, to encourage involvement.

- Engagement of community supporters.

It would be naïve to assume that the mere existence of successful strategies can lead to the bridging of the Achievement Gap. The stories told in this book are the exceptions. Few people beyond the world of professional educators and the families who send their children to excellent schools know much about their existence. A more typical point of view can be found in newspaper articles such as one titled, "Familiar Story in State Test Scores," from the September 28, 2017, edition of the San Francisco Chronicle:

> "Every year, education officials release standardized test scores, and every year they say the same thing: the Achievement Gap persists. This year's scores are no different."

The story continued, "Despite decades of effort and billions of dollars in funding, test scores for White, Asian American and wealthier students are much higher than those for their Black, Latino and low-income peers. On computerized tests administered in the spring, for example, just 19 percent of African American students were proficient in math, compared to 73 percent of Asian American students."

The schools examined in the Second Edition are exceptional in many ways, but not because they have extraordinary financial resources. Most of the schools are charter schools – public schools for which parents make some sacrifices for their children to attend.

Charter schools can be controversial. They capture attendance dollars that would otherwise be directed toward traditional schools. They often operate without collective bargaining agreements for employees. Charter schools come in many models, and some have been financial and academic failures. My focus has been on successful public charters, operated either by Charter Management Organizations or run independently in cooperation with a school district and a community.

We must remember most controversies about charter schools involve political themes and professional issues. Those issues tend to focus not on children, but on special-interest considerations, such as school district funding and union representation. Those are important discussions, but they are not part of my examination of bridging the Achievement Gap. My concern here is for African American children and their families. They are my special interest.

Accordingly, the opportunity for African American parents to send their children to a charter school that best serves their needs should not be impeded by policies that fail to benefit these children and their families.

State propositions, or legislation designed to place a cap on the growth of charter schools, must be vehemently opposed. Consider the timeless law of the marketplace. If a traditional school meets a parent's needs, that parent will not make the effort to enroll their children in a charter school. Parents know when they and their children are valued – or not. They recognize when their children are learning – or not. They realize when they are simply being passed along year after year – when their children fail to be adequately prepared for college or careers. So please, let's continue to give African American parents a choice!

As I wrote in 2011 at the conclusion of Chapter Five in the First Edition, "It takes more than a simple declaration to start up a new school or to restructure an existing one. Key leaders must be fully committed to do whatever it takes to implement their goals successfully." Today, that observation continues and is no less relevant for planners of an individual school. But let us consider recommendations at another level.

Clearly, there should be policy decisions made among senior statewide authorities to embrace the best practices described here and bridge the Achievement Gap at scale. To achieve this goal, my recommendation is to focus on raising the levels of proficiency for the lowest-achieving students in English Language Arts and mathematics. Historically, African American students have been the lowest-performing subgroup, other than students with special needs, in state assessments for English Language Arts and Math. Statewide, African American students who are not categorized as low income still achieve at similar or lower levels than their low-income white peers. Given these realities, a unified effort to bring scale to practices that will close the Achievement Gap should include all African American students, including those who may not live in low-income households.

In California, Governor Jerry Brown, the State Legislature and the State Board of Education created major changes in the K-12 education system in 2013. They eliminated the use of the Academic Performance Index as a measure of school status. They changed the state testing instruments for elementary and secondary students.

They advocated for the inclusion California Common Core State Standards as a replacement for Content Standards. They required local school districts to produce Local Control Accountability Plans (LCAP), which describe how their goals would be achieved. Finally, they changed the financing of schools and school districts with the Local Control Funding Formula. The new formula provides resources for all students attending elementary, middle and high schools, and gives supplemental money for children defined as "high needs" students.

Under the rules, three subgroups of students with high needs receive extra funds: low income, English learners, and foster youth. African American students who underperform are not designated as "high needs," unless they are low income, English learners, or in foster care. Thus, distribution of funds within those three groups excludes about 90,000 African American public school children in California. Each day, in schools across the state, the system fails many of those 90,000 students.

Beyond the benefits of more state funding, why would it matter if all African American students in California were identified as "high needs" students? Let's return to the Local Control and Accountability Plans, or LCAP. Under the rules governing LCAP, public schools are required to develop, implement and evaluate educational supports for students who are designated as "high needs." If African American students were identified as "high needs," public schools in California would be required to create specific plans for how to better serve African American students.

Let's remember, African American students are the lowest-performing subgroup outside of students with special needs. Our students can be referred to as such, without making any reference to race, to alleviate concerns about compliance with Proposition 209. Of course, we can hope that with time, hard work and investment, distinctions such as "high needs" will no longer be needed to describe thousands of African American students. That would be progress – a true success story. Resources and attention could then shift to other children with high needs.

But currently, and aside from political arguments and semantics, one truth remains: any subgroup that consistently performs lowest on state standardized tests is clearly "high needs," and should be recognized and given extra financial support and attention, mandated by law and policy from state and local levels. Without such recognition, the Achievement Gap will continue to grow.

In recognition of these realities, I have joined with other educators to recommend an amendment to California Education Code 42238.02. The amendment would create an additional "high needs" group within the Local Control Funding Formula (LCFF). Please note the proposed new language under Section (E):

Amend Education Code 42238.02.

(b) (1) For the purposes of this section "unduplicated pupil" means a pupil enrolled in a school district or a charter school who is either classified as an English learner; eligible for a free or reduce-price meal; a member of the lowest performing subgroup, excluding the students with disabilities subgroup on state assessments; or is a foster youth. A pupil shall be counted only once for purposes of this section if any of the following apply:

(A) The pupil classified as an English learner and is eligible for a free or reduced-price meal.

(B) The pupil is classified as an English learner and is a foster youth.

(C) The pupil is eligible for a free or reduced-price meal and is classified as foster youth.

(D) The pupil is classified as an English learner and is eligible for a free or reduced price meal and is a foster youth.

(E) Commencing with the 2018-19 fiscal year, "unduplicated pupil" shall also mean a pupil who is included in the lowest performing subgroup or subgroups, as defined in Section 52052, based on the most recently available mathematics or language arts results on the California Assessment of Student Performance and Progress. For the purposes of this paragraph, the Superintendent shall annually identify the lowest performing pupil subgroup or subgroups.

Three members of the California State Assembly, Shirley Weber (D-San Diego), Mike Gipson (D-Gardena) and Autumn Burke (D-Inglewood), have introduced as Assembly Bill 2635, which will enact this language.

Should AB 2635 become law, school districts and school leaders will be expected to implement the new language – and fulfill its intent. To simply receive more funds and continue current programs of instructions, counseling and career training will likely produce no changes to the Achievement Gap, or improve college readiness.

Alternatively, if local school leaders carefully examine their personnel selections, amounts of instructional time, extra support and parental involvement at schools that are successful with the population of students who are generally low achieving, California can make real progress toward bridging the Achievement Gap.

If the legislation does not become law, school districts and site leaders should still examine the strategies of successful schools described in Chapter One. These are places where our students thrive every day. Moreover, school and community leaders should determine how they can improve their own programs. If state and local conversations around this legislative proposal result in a greater effort to replicate the best practices, then the work for a solution at the State Capitol will have not been in vain.

Successful legislation requires a political willingness to work together and compromise. I hope such willingness exists in Sacramento, but even if it does not, there are several recommendations school leaders should consider to bridge the Achievement Gap. I've listed five basic actions to encourage the conversation and help the march toward progress:

1. Launch an effective "cradle to career" approach to dramatically improve the achievement of African American students.

2. Improve every parent's ability to assist their children at home and to become critical partners at school.

3. Harness programs and services of existing civic and cultural organizations, churches, business and other community-based organizations to help African American learners of all age groups.

4. Adopt research-based ideas and suggestions from schools that already have implemented successful practices for African American students.

5. Conduct credible evaluations and publish strategies that work.

California continues to become more diversified, as reflected in its student population in 2016, where 54 percent of children were Latino, 24 percent white, 9 percent Asian and 6 percent African American. Educators and policy makers must find ways for all subgroups to experience success in education and career development at the elementary, middle and high school levels.

Every key indicator – test scores, graduation rates, "A-to-G" course completion rates for public university eligibility, college admission rates, college graduation rates, suspension rates, incarceration rates – all suggest we have much work to do. A single piece of legislation, a few words written into law, can't resolve generations of disparity, prejudice and neglect. But we should expect educational leaders to seize every opportunity to move us along the path toward progress.

Remember the words of the late Dr. Ronald Edmonds:

"We can, whenever and wherever we choose, successfully teach all children whose schooling is of interest to us. Whether or not we do this, depends upon how we feel about the fact that we haven't done it so far."

Baldwin Hills Principal Letitia Johnson-Davis

PS 7 Principal Kari Wehrly

Wilder Prep team with author, left to right: Kimberly Paggett-Willis, Ramona Wilder, Rex Fortune, Carolyn Wilder, Rosalyn Robinson, Germaine Jackson

Watts Learning Center

KIPP Scholar Principal Tiffany Moore

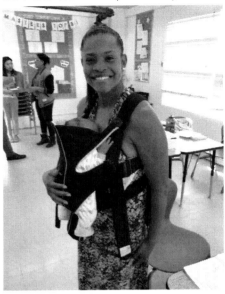

KIPP Scholar student

Sacramento High Principal Shannon Wheatley

Oak Park Prep Principal Annie Cervenka

Margaret S. Fortune, left, with Odisa Nyong, former principal of Fortune School and current principal of the Rex & Margaret Fortune Early College High School.

Appendix

Methodology

A. Selections of High-Performing, Mostly African American Schools

Three criteria were used to identify which public schools in California were closing the achievement gap in 2015-2017. First, at least half of any school's test-takers had to be African American. Second, schools needed to rank at least a five out of 10 in terms of pure academic achievement on a statewide basis. (In other words, at least near the state average.) Third, schools needed to rank 10 out of 10 in terms of demographic-adjusted achievement on a statewide basis. (In other words, in the top 10 percent of schools after considering their student demographics.) In 2016 and 2017, these criteria identified a dozen schools. Five schools appear on the list in both years, resulting in 19 unique schools. This book contains information about 11 of those 19 schools, including four that are on the list in both years: Fortune School, KIPP Empower, Watts Learning Center, and Wilder's Preparatory Academy.

We obtained all data from the research files on the California Assessment of Student Performance and Progress (CAASPP) website, available here:

https://caaspp.cde.ca.gov/sb2017/ResearchFileList.
We used the following methods:

— To calculate the percent African American, we used the "Students with Scores in Grade" for all students (grade 13), dividing the number for African American students (subgroup 74) by all students (subgroup 1).

— To determine state rank, we created a school-wide "distance from level 3" score for all schools. This required calculating a "distance from level 3 score" for each grade, and then taking a weighted average of all tested grades in a school. We then removed schools that had fewer than 30 students with scores, as well as schools that participated in the Alternative Schools Accountability Model (ASAM) program in 2014-15. We sorted the remaining schools into equal-sized bins from 1 (lowest) to 10 (highest) and called this the state rank.

— To determine similar school rank, we calculated the difference between each school's actual average scale score and the score we would predict based on student demographics. First, we ran regressions at each grade level and subject where the dependent variable was "average scale score" and the independent variables were an array of factors that schools cannot control. We used these regressions to generate predicted scores, which we subtracted from the actual average scale scores. Lastly, we took the weighted average of all grades in each school to create one "actual minus predicted" score, and ranked schools from 1 to 10.

The results for two years beginning in 2016 show 12 schools whose English Language Arts scores are above the African American statewide average score of 31 percent. Of those schools, six have ELA proficiency above the statewide average for all students at 49 percent.

Figure 1:

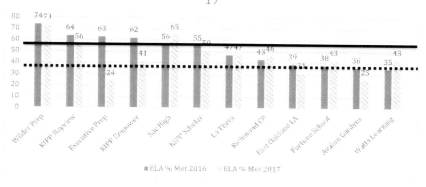

2016 List: ELA % Met on CAASPP 2015-16 and 2016-17

Figure 2:

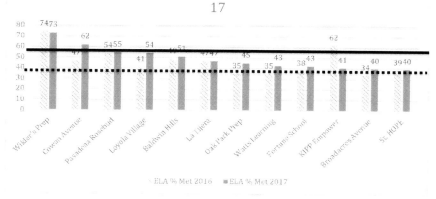

2017 List: ELA % Met on CAASPP 2015-16 and 2016-17

In this set of schools, all scored above the statewide average proficiency in ELA for African American students at 31 percent, and five scored above the statewide average proficiency in ELA for all students at 49 percent.

Figure 3:

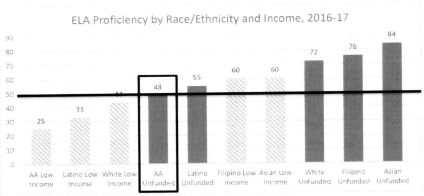

ELA Proficiency by Race/Ethnicity and Income, 2016-17

B. Middle-Class, Lower-Performing African American Students are a High-Need Group

The graph above showing levels of proficiency by ethnic group by income level shows low-income students with slanted lines and unfunded (that is, not low-income) students with solid bars. Low-income students receive supplemental funding in the LCFF formula, but while other students do not, unless they are English Learners. While a significant number of Latino students are English Learners, very few African American students are categorized as EL. From the graph, it is apparent that while non-low-income African American students do not receive funding, their level of proficiency is lower than some students who receive funding due to low incomes. As the performance of African Americans on the CAASPP ELA is lower than the statewide average, the middle-class African American is therefore a high-need group. This analysis is the basis for the remedy specified in AB 2635 and discussed in Chapter Five.

Figures 4a and 4b: Data on High Performing African American California Schools for 2016-17

School	District	% African American	% Proficient in English	% Proficient in Math	Charter School?
Wilder's Prep Academy	Inglewood	87	69	61	Yes
Cowan Avenue Elementary	Los Angeles	87	62	52	No
KIPP Empower Academy	Los Angeles	71	41	52	Yes
Pasadena Rosebud Academy	Pasadena	75	55	48	Yes
Loyola Village Magnet	Los Angeles	52	54	34	No
Watts Learning Center	Los Angeles	50	43	44	Yes
Baldwin Hills Elementary	Los Angeles	85	51	35	No
Braodacres Avenue Elementary	Los Angeles	79	40	46	No
La Tijera K-8 Academy	Inglewood	60	47	23	Yes
Fortune School	Sacramento	55	43	36	Yes
Oak Park Preparatory Academy	Sacramento	63	45	41	Yes
ST HOPE Public Schools	Sacramento	60	40	34	Yes
	State Average for All Students		49	38	
	State Average for African American Students		31	19	

2016 CAASPP DATA

School	District	% African American	% Proficient in English	% Proficient in Math	Charter School?
KIPP Bay View (5-8)	San Francisco	51	64	37	Yes
KPP Scholar (5-8)	Los Angeles	54	55	32	Yes
Sacramento High	Sacramento	66	56	23	Yes

School Enrollment	Similar School Ranking	State Rank	All students ELA % Met	All Students Math % Met	African American ELA % Met	African American Math % Met
Baldwin Hills Elementary 378	10	6	51	35	49	34
Broadacres Avenue Elementary 303	10	6	40	46	40	48
Cowan Avenue Elementary 296	10	8	62	52	59	49
Fortune School 360	10	5	43	36	39	32
KIPP Empower Academy 563	10	7	41	52	40	49
La Tijera K-8 Academy of Excel 704	10	5	47	23	47	22
Loyola Village Arts Magnet 395	10	7	54	34	50	30
Oak Park Preparatory Academy 138	10	5	45	41	34	33
Pasadena Rosebud Academy 152	10	7	55	48	51	39
St. HOPE Public School 7 565	10	5	40	34	36	27
Watts Learning Center 367	10	6	43	44	33	35
Wilder's Prep Academy Charter 567	10	9	72	52	72	53

State-Level

All students ELA % Met	All Students Math % Met	African American ELA % Met	African American Math % Met
49	38	31	19

C. National Assessment of Educational Progress Scores

African Americans are the lowest-performing ethnic group nationally. (Figures from 2013, most recent data available.) Figures 5 and 6:

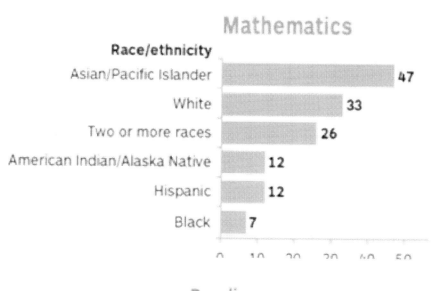

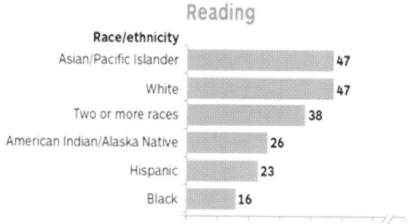

About the Authors

Rex Fortune

Father, husband, teacher, and businessman with a passion for bridging the Achievement Gap, Fortune has worked more than 50 years as an educator. He was a high school teacher, school site administrator, associate superintendent of public instruction in the California State Department of Education for 11 years, superintendent of Inglewood Unified School District for five years, and superintendent of Center Unified School District for 15 years before he retired from Center in 2003. He received his B.S. and U.S. Army commission from North Carolina A&T State University in 1962, an M.A. from UC Berkeley in 1968, and a Ph.D from Stanford University in 1972. While leading Center Unified, Fortune founded the Fortune School of Education,

AKA Project Pipeline, in 1989. He served as past president of the Board of Trustees for the Fortune School of Education and the Pacific Charter Institute, which governs charter schools in Sacramento and San Joaquin counties. This second edition of *Bridging the Achievement Gap: What Successful Educators and Parents Do* is his fifth book on education. He lives in Granite Bay, California.

Dominic Zarecki

Senior Data Analyst at Fortune School of Education. Zarecki provides technical and research assistance to the central office, helps teachers navigate data systems and evaluates the effectiveness of interventions. Before working at Fortune School of Education, Zarecki was Director of Research at the California Charter Schools Association, where he helped implement and update a statewide accountability system and wrote reports about the academic and post-secondary performance of charter schools. He is on the Technical Design Group, which advises the California Department of Education about statistical issues related to its accountability work, and a member of Cohort 8 of the Strategic Data Project, a two-year fellowship based in the Center for Education Policy Research at Harvard University. Dominic earned a doctorate and M.A. in Political Science from Boston University and a B.A. from Yale University. He resides in Riverside, California.

Rex Fortune III

Vice President of Fortune and Associates for the past decade. Previously, Rex III worked 12 years as a Director of Teacher Recruitment and Marketing; a Teacher Training Program Coordinator for the Contra Costa County program he initiated; and a Facilities and Events Coordinator for Project Pipeline Teacher Credential Program, now called the Fortune School of Education. For Fortune and Associates, Rex III did most of the logistics associated with the first edition of this book, including research of API test scores for over 10,000 California public schools, to choose the 20 best schools that met the criteria for the study. He wrote the script for the book's corresponding DVD, *Parenting Practices: How Successful Parents Bridge the Achievement Gap*. He assisted with the logistics and write-ups for interviews with educators and parents at selected schools included in the second edition. Rex III has a bachelor's degree in human resources, specializing in training and development, from the California Polytechnic State University in Pomona. He lives in Granite Bay, California.

Acknowledgements

First, I want to thank the principals, teachers, and parents of the schools we visited who shared their time and insights about ways they helped their students become high achievers. Appreciation is extended to school secretaries or office managers who facilitated the creation of schedules for school visits and enabled our data collection.

Secondly, I want to acknowledge the able and creative editorial work of R.E. Graswich. Robert enlivened the stories about the schools in this study, based upon my reports of school practices. Communications with Robert were always easy, even though most of them were by email or phone. I think we only had three face-to-face meetings, which were very productive.

Next, the staff at the Fortune School of Education was critical in a variety of ways. Margaret Fortune, President and CEO of the Fortune School of Education and President of the California Charter School Associations Board, saw early on a connection between the mission of the California Charter Schools Association to expand the growth of effective charter schools in California and the need to find examples of charter schools that were particularly effective with the lowest performing students on the statewide CAASPP tests in English Language Arts and mathematics. She enabled a few of her Fortune School of Education staff to participate in the early phases of the design of the study for the book. Matt Taylor, Director of Data Analysis, Dr. Dominic Zarecki, Senior Data Analyst, Dr. Kristy Pruitt, Director of Teacher Education, and Vanessa Caigoy, Coordinator of Compliance for state and federal programs, were helpful in that process. Taylor and Dr. Zarecki provided useful insights regarding statewide student performance data pertaining to major student groups, including: Asian American, African American, Hispanic and white students. Their work was reflected in certain details associated with AB 2635 described in "Chapter Five: the Solution," as well as in the methodology discussed in the Appendix. I want also acknowledge assistance provided by Elva Lopez and Marquita Jones, administrative assistants, who have rescued me from a number of technology traps associated with the production and transmittal of drafts.

Thirdly, I want to acknowledge the on-going assistance of Rex Fortune III, Vice President of Fortune and Associates, who helped plan all aspects for this research. In addition to making air and ground travel arrangements as well as lodging for our travels, Rex III visited several schools with me. He recorded interviews, took photos, and proofread initial draft reports of schools visits. Rex III has been instrumental in virtually every aspect of producing the book, including editing, printing and publication. As he has been an integral part of the production and sales of other Fortune & Associates products, including DVDs, videos and website re-design, his work on this publication is often sandwiched between other high-priority projects. His ability to multi-task has been a valuable aspect of this work.

I want to thank Dr. Anette Melvin for her thorough editing of the final draft of the Second Edition. Her sharp eye made significant improvements to the final product.

As usual, my wife, Margaret S. Fortune endured many intrusions on our retirement planning during the writing of this book. Her patience and encouragement continue to enable me to undertake projects such as this research. I want her to know how valuable that is to me.

Rex Fortune
Granite Bay, California
June 2018

Index